# PERGAMON INTERNATIONAL LIBRARY
## of Science, Technology, Engineering and Social Studies

*The 1000-volume original paperback library in aid of education,
industrial training and the enjoyment of leisure*

Publisher: Robert Maxwell, M.C.

# The Sister Bond

## THE PERGAMON TEXTBOOK
## INSPECTION COPY SERVICE

An inspection copy of any book published in the Pergamon International Library
will gladly be sent to academic staff without obligation for their consideration for
course adoption or recommendation. Copies may be retained for a period of 60 days
from receipt and returned if not suitable. When a particular title is adopted or
recommended for adoption for class use and the recommendation results in a sale
of 12 or more copies the inspection copy may be retained with our compliments.
The Publishers will be pleased to receive suggestions for revised editions and new
titles to be published in this important international Library.

**THE ATHENE SERIES**
An International Collection of Feminist Books
*General Editors:* Gloria Bowles and Renate Duelli-Klein
*Consulting Editor:* Dale Spender

---

The ATHENE SERIES assumes that all those who are concerned with formulating explanations of the way the world works need to know and appreciate the significance of basic feminist principles.

The growth of feminist research has challenged almost all aspects of social organization in our culture. The ATHENE SERIES focuses on the construction of knowledge and the exclusion of women from the process — both as theorists and subjects of study—and offers innovative studies that challenge established theories and research.

---

**ON ATHENE** — When Metis, goddess of wisdom who presided over all knowledge was pregnant with ATHENE, she was swallowed up by Zeus who then gave birth to ATHENE from his head. The original ATHENE is thus the parthenogenetic daughter of a strong mother and as the feminist myth goes, at the "third birth" of ATHENE she stops being Zeus' obedient mouthpiece and returns to her real source: the science and wisdom of womankind

---

**Volumes in the Series**

MEN'S STUDIES MODIFIED  The Impact of Feminism
on the Academic Disciplines
*edited by* Dale Spender

MACHINA EX DEA  Feminist Perspectives on Technology
*edited by* Joan Rothschild

WOMEN'S NATURE  Rationalizations of Inequality
*edited by* Marian Lowe and Ruth Hubbard

SCIENCE AND GENDER  A Critique of Biology and Its Theories on Women
Ruth Bleier

WOMAN IN THE MUSLIM UNCONSCIOUS
Fatna A. Sabbah

MEN'S IDEAS/WOMEN'S REALITIES  *Popular Science,* 1870-1915
*edited by* Louise Michele Newman

BLACK FEMINIST CRITICISM  Perspectives on Black Women Writers
Barbara Christian

THE SISTER BOND  A Feminist View of a Timeless Connection
*edited by* Toni A.H. McNaron

NOTICE TO READERS

May we suggest that your library places a standing/continuation order to receive all future volumes in the Athene Series immediately on publication?
Your order can be cancelled at any time.

**Also of Interest**
WOMEN'S STUDIES INTERNATIONAL FORUM*
*Editor:* Dale Spender
*\*Free sample copy available on request*

# The Sister Bond

A Feminist View of a Timeless Connection

*edited by* Toni A.H. McNaron
*University of Minnesota*

**Pergamon Press**

New York • Oxford • Toronto • Sydney • Paris • Frankfurt

Pergamon Press Offices:

| | |
|---|---|
| **U.S.A.** | Pergamon Press Inc., Maxwell House, Fairview Park, Elmsford, New York 10523, U.S.A. |
| **U.K.** | Pergamon Press Ltd., Headington Hill Hall, Oxford OX3 0BW, England |
| **CANADA** | Pergamon Press Canada Ltd., Suite 104, 150 Consumers Road, Willowdale, Ontario M2J 1P9, Canada |
| **AUSTRALIA** | Pergamon Press (Aust.) Pty. Ltd., P.O. Box 544, Potts Point, NSW 2011, Australia |
| **FRANCE** | Pergamon Press SARL, 24 rue des Ecoles, 75240 Paris, Cedex 05, France |
| **FEDERAL REPUBLIC OF GERMANY** | Pergamon Press GmbH, Hammerweg 6, D-6242 Kronberg-Taunus, Federal Republic of Germany |

**Library of Congress Cataloging in Publication Data**
Main entry under title:
The Sister bond.
(The Athene series)
Includes index.
1. Sisters-England—Addresses, essays, lectures.
2. Sisters—United States—Addresses, essays,
lectures. 3 Women authors, English—Biography—
Addresses, essays, lectures. 4. Women authors,
American—Biography—Addresses, essays, lectures.
5. Sisters in literature—Addresses, essays, lectures.
I. McNaron, Toni A. H. II. Series.
HQ1599.E5S57 1985 306.8'754 85-3477
ISBN 0-08-032367-7 (Hardcover)
ISBN 0-08-032366-9 (Flexicover)

*Printed in Great Britain by A. Wheaton & Co. Ltd., Exeter*

# Contents

# Acknowledgments

I wish to thank Dale Spender for the initial suggestion to make a book on the subject of blood sisters, Madelon Sprengnether and Shirley Garner for their constant support during the writing and preparation of the manuscript, Sunny Steinmetz for her fast and dependable typing of the entire manuscript, and the members of my women's writing group for their trenchant suggestions for revision of the introduction.

I especially want to thank Susan Cygnet for her meticulous proofreading of the final copies of the essays and, more importantly, for her steadiness during various crises such as my losing essays momentarily and drifting in and out of hysterics during the last few weeks before shipping the manuscript to the publisher.

Finally, I want to thank my own blood sister, Betty, without whose existence, the entire subject would have remained academic for me.

# 1 How Little We Know and How Much We Feel

Toni A. H. McNaron

Sisters: two or more women, related by blood, adoption, marriage, or religious commitment and service; or, large groups of women drawn together by bonds of feminist thought and practice. For the purposes of this collection, I use the term to refer to two women related by blood, most often growing up in the same house, in the same room, often sleeping in the same bed. As are all women, such sisters are taught by literature and culture to compete for the attention of men, beginning often with their father. Yet when asked to speak about their connections with each other, members of these pairs usually find themselves articulating a deep and turbulent bond, one that precedes and outlasts friendships, courtships, even marriages. A search of the literature reveals almost no work on this subject. Aside from Louise Bernikow's brave words in her chapter "Sometimes I feel like a sisterless child" (*Among Women*, Harper & Row, 1980), I find only an occasional poem or novel about the tangle of sisterhood. As with the examination of the mother-daughter bond that began a few years ago, the best source of information remains primary documents by the women themselves or the rare biography that treats their relationship seriously.

I began this book because I believed it would shed light on my checkered relationship with my own sister. Separated by sixteen years, she and I seem worlds apart in our attitudes, interests, and modes of living. The tension and charge that exist between us are too severe and explosive to be explained by a recital of those attitudes or interests. When I was a child and looked at her, a college coed, I did not see myself in any literal sense. If anything, I saw another mother and she, looking back at me, saw a child young enough to be hers. But our dynamic is not that of surrogate mother-daughter; our connection resembles that expressed by scores of women speaking about their sisters. I feel closer to her on some psychic level than to any friends or lovers; I yearn for a kind of exchange that is not possible without our becoming the same person. The extreme loneliness that results pains me more than I like to admit.

No matter how much we disagree, I cannot close the book on my sister. Though I feel sad and angry when I can't get more of what I want from her, I am not prepared to say "Well, that's the way it is. I can't make her into someone she isn't any more than I can be what she truly would like in a sister." To do that would be to erase the part of myself that resides in her — the articulate, stylish, fragile-but-willful daughter of a Southern belle. I refused or was constitutionally unable to develop those aspects of myself, even though

3

I knew them to lurk inside me. My fantasy self, who always caused me to feel inadequate, was tall, slim, a rider of horses and player of bridge named Hurley, my mother's maiden name. While my sister does not literally fit this description, her role in our family most nearly approximates this fictitious female. I, on the other hand, am the shortish, stocky, outwardly-tough-but-truly-sentimental daughter, whose artist-mother, lacking a medium, was driven toward beauty in all her domestic labor.

The name I answer to, "Toni," was given me *in utero*, not by my parents, but by my sister. She chose a neutral name that would serve equally well regardless of my gender. I thank her in retrospect for doing this, since I believe my name helped me resist the heavy socialization into the feminine roles of my culture. But the single most important "gift" from my sister came unwittingly, I believe. Except for the few months of her first marriage, she stayed home for all of our mother's life. Contrarily, I began getting away through fantasy games and worlds I invented in childhood and left physically at the first opportunity, when I was seventeen and off to college. Though there was love and support at home, I felt closed in and overseen. I have had to deal with guilt for leaving my mother in her times of need, but the fact that I have gone ahead and done it has depended largely on my sister. She discovered that she was not happy living anywhere but with her mother, and so continued to do that until death intervened. Since my blood sister was fulfilling the role of dutiful daughter, I was free to develop that part of myself that yearned for independence and adventure. We never spoke of this, but I am clear that I profited from our difference. I sometimes wonder if she did not also benefit.

In an attempt to make sense out of the life-long struggle and devotion between Virginia Stephen (Woolf) and her sister, Vanessa Stephen (Bell), I wrote an essay that was to form the nucleus for this book. I quickly found that their lives resembled my own with my sister. In the stories found in the essays that follow, some version of this phenomenon recurs with startling regularity. Either one sister encourages the other to play out some complementary self that she does not or cannot become, or forces around them are such that complementarity becomes the pattern within which both act out their adult lives. It is as though unconsciously the pairs, including my sister and me, evolve a system in which they develop only certain parts of themselves in order to cut down on or avoid altogether the powerful pulls toward competition found within virtually any family.

Once my essay about Virginia and Vanessa Stephen was completed, I was convinced that what I'd found to exist between these two upper middle-class English women, growing up at the turn of the twentieth century, could be duplicated or enlarged upon if we only could know more stories. The pairs included here are in many cases expected subjects for such a work: the Austens, the Stephens, the Dickinsons. Others are included because their stories are powerful and instructive, if at times painful, e.g., the Wrights, the Nightingales, the Abbotts. Still others offer paradigms for countless sisters living in the late nineteenth and twentieth centuries, e.g., the Rossettis, the Levertovs, the Richs.

All the sisters written about in this collection are English or American, middle-class, white women. They were educated from their father's libraries if not at colleges; at least one of each pair achieved some degree of public notice during her lifetime or, in the case of Emily Dickinson, posthumously. It is a serious weakness of this collection that it does not include the lives of Black sisters, sisters from Continental or Third World cultures, and those from diverse class backgrounds. I made extensive efforts to find work on such women, but none was forthcoming. Part of the problem has its locus in racism and class bias as they figure in the preservation of information. If it is hard to find out about white, middle-class women because we live in a patriarchy, it is doubly hard to learn of Black or working-class women. Records barely exist if a female child from such surroundings has made a name for herself; certainly a less public sister would have faded into oblivion long ago. This book is meant as a step on the way to filling out our picture of sisterhood as feminists come to define a female sphere.

The relationship between sisters, like that between mothers and daughters, comes to us shrouded in silence and ignorance. Like mothers and daughters, sisters are by definition a woman-to-woman dyad and, as such, may well constitute a threat within patriarchy. Any social grouping that does not include at least one male figure tends to cause questions, uneasiness, even fear. A culture dependent upon everyone's accepting male superiority cannot handle maleless relationships calmly. This potential threat partially explains the distorted depictions, by women and men alike, of sisters as yipping shrews or colorless maidens. It also suggests reasons for the widespread avoidance of the subject. In the interpretation of the sister bond that follows, I speak from personal experience as well as from conversation with many women about their sisters. The correspondence between our contemporary feelings and the stories included here is striking, even though I realize that many sisters in the present and in our past could not agree with my reading of this connection.

In the past decade, much feminist research and writing has gone toward increasing our knowledge and understanding of the troubled and potent matrix that exists between mothers and daughters. Thanks to such writers as Nancy Chodorow (*The Reproduction of Mothering: Psychoanalysis and the Sociology of Gender*, University of California Press, Berkeley, 1978) and Adrienne Rich (*Of Woman Born: Motherhood as Experience and Institution*, W. W. Norton & Company, New York, 1976), it is no longer shocking to assert that a mother is her daughter's first lover as surely as she is her son's.

Both scholars point out the nearly impossible task of separation that lies before a young woman as she attempts to become culturally acceptable in her adult sexuality. A boy can continue to choose sexual partners who resemble his mother and still gain social approval, but a girl pays for her hetero-sexuality. And if she continues to love women's bodies, not only must she cope with external censure, but also with her own confusion about identity as an adult. Lesbians who consider this problem admit that having one's lover look like one's first source of sensual and physical security and pleasure complicates lovemaking even if it deepens emotional and spiritual connections. A fundamental approach-avoidance pattern sets in, made strong by the incest taboo; intimacy is then as often feared as desired.

Girl children have difficulty in establishing boundaries between themselves and the person of the (m)other. Chodorow postulates that, during infancy, such babies have felt a total blurring of self into other, and that monumental fact cannot be completely wiped out or "grown out of." Consequently, adult females often have intense ambivalence toward their own bodies and toward their mothers, who they feel alternately suffocated them with sameness and refused them the total union they wanted. Rich argues movingly that the socialization process which forces young women into compulsory heterosexuality costs them close friendships and intimacies with adult women throughout their lives.

Since blood sisters participate in a woman-to-woman bond, made even more powerful by their being from the same parents, I find it useful to think of this couple as having the potential for being each other's second lovers, since their common mother is their shared first lover. Each sister perceives her sibling as primary to her own definition of intimacy within the family. Whether their bond remains emotional or extends itself to physical interaction, the two make a fierce pact at an early stage of their development. This fact may have as much to do with later feelings of competition and jealousy as any culturally instilled messages about women's fighting over the same man. In fact, our heterosexual myopia may have led us to overlook the possibility that sisters, when they are jealous over a parent, may well be jealous over their mother. In any event, their strong and in some instances inexplicable feelings for each other certainly pre-date any potential struggle over a father's affection and attention.

This primacy of the sister can be seen in as unlikely a place as the supposed novels of manners written by Jane Austen. In many of her works, Austen chose sisters as a key subtext. In *Pride and Prejudice*, for instance, we find that before Elizabeth Bennett can soften her prejudice toward the proud Mr. Darcey, he must rescue her younger sister from her spoiled reputation as mistress of the roue/soldier Wickham. In the same novel, Elizabeth and her sister Jane confide their troubles over Darcey and Bingley, Jane's preferred, with one another rather than with either parent. At the end of the story, the two men, who are devoted friends, are manipulated by the author until they both decide to ask for the hands of this close-knit pair. As a reader, I at least assume that these heterosexual couples will spend much time with each other; thus continuation of the primary bond between the sisters is in no way jeopardized by conventional marriages.

A sister can be seen as someone who is both ourselves and very much not ourselves — a special kind of double. The phenomenon of identical twin girls makes this assertion the most comprehensible. Twins have told me that each sibling literally sees herself when she looks at the other. This mirror effect blurs emotional and psychological boundaries. Such a total identification, often buttressed by parents who insist on dressing the pair in the same clothes, surely makes more complex the arduous task of forming an authentic sense of identity. Consequently a situation that involves tremendous intimacy can also elicit fierce confusion. Any one of us can easily project onto someone else those parts of ourselves that we do not want to incorporate into our own sense of self. Given this psychodynamic, I would posit that twin sisters must work unusually hard to learn to take individual responsibility for their own personalities. Having a look-alike would make it so easy to displace one's own less pleasing characteristics onto one's twin.

Questions of whether and how to form bonds of intimacy are more difficult to answer in such cases, but I believe that many sisters find such connections problematic. Though the closer the two girls are in ages, the more nearly their struggle to distinguish self from other may approach that of twins. Age in itself, however, will not erase the dilemma. In my own case, my sister and I are separated by many years. Yet I have experienced a similar dilemma in seeing myself as distinct from her.

I am convinced that the dynamic sketched above results from something essential within the sister-bond, unexamined and unnamed. The desire to be one, juxtaposed against the necessity to be two, lies at the heart of this mystery. The sisters spoken about in this collection have stories whose plotlines present us useful insights. In some cases, the two women never overtly express the depth of their feelings for one another, while in others, the language that surrounds them forces us to acknowledge the closeness. Sisters speak of being "wedded" to one another, of being "irreplaceable" in one another's lives, of caring in ways that lie beyond the limits of socially defined sisterhood. When one sister dies, the other is often lost and confused by unresolvable feelings that hasten her own demise or actual death. If sisters become estranged, their letters and diaries reflect great pain and longing, a sense of having been split from themselves violently, inexplicably. When such estrangements can be healed, the joy and relief often equals the earlier despondent and/or destructive feelings. Even when one sister senses that resolution will not be forthcoming, the struggle to figure out the rift, to work out the damage, goes on until something changes or some peace is achieved. Denise Levertov provides an excellent example of this process of working it out: she seems unable to rest until she has found a way to merge again with her sister's "eyes" that continue to haunt her.

The other phenomenon traced in most of the pairs included here is the unspoken, probably unconscious, pact that neither sister need develop all her potential. Living as closely as most sisters do, each can see some of herself being acted out by her sibling. Where this occurs, each sister comes to depend upon the other to continue to act in certain ways. Had my own sister decided to leave home while I was pursuing my life and career miles away, a silent but crucial balance would have been upset. Even if I had not changed my plans and returned home, I would most certainly have felt tremendous guilt and discomfort for continuing to live independently. So it appears in many of the pairs found here. If anyone crosses over an invisible, necessary line that may be of many years duration, both sisters could well find the result frightening and a threat to their autonomy and very sense of themselves. So Emily Dickinson liked to believe that her sister Lavinia was the one who enjoyed domestic chores — sweeping the floors, trotting out to fill shopping orders, baking little cakes and pastries, tending their ailing mother with a real will. She cast herself, on the other hand, as requiring solitude, time to compose her poetry and be in touch with her deepest sources. What must she have felt, knowing that in reality Lavinia was one of her most rigorous critics while she herself loved to bake loaves of bread each week? We may never know the answers to these questions for Emily Dickinson, but surely we might posit tentative responses for sisters currently alive if feminists and others took up the subject of sister bonds with the seriousness it warrants.

The women discussed in this volume fall roughly into two groups: those who used each other as a repository for troublesome or painful aspects of self; those who saw in their relationship with each other a chance to comprehend an expanded self. The clearest example of the former is Fanny and Camilla Wright. As the mutually accepted leader, Fanny pushed off onto Camilla her softer, more domestic self because to own it would have made much more difficult her life as a public figure. Seeing such emotions and activities as either pedestrian or crippling, Fanny put a wide berth between herself and her adoring sister. For her own part, Camilla was willing to endure this oversimplification of herself in order to remain close to her idol. As Celia Eckhardt has sensitively shown, "life for her [Camilla] became unthinkable apart from Fanny's." Camilla went where Fanny did and performed whatever function Fanny asked of her, even when doing so was at her own expense. A poignant example of the lengths to which Camilla would go is found in Eckhardt's account of Camilla's reaction to trans-Atlantic travel. On their first voyage, she was so violently and unrelentingly seasick that her horror of ocean voyages never left her. Yet she embarked on the tortuous thirty-day journey repeatedly because Fanny needed to be in England or on the Continent to further her political career.

However, Fanny knew what she was asking; she also understood that Camilla gave her the "devotion that undergirded the psychic strength Fanny needed to break one taboo after another." Eckhardt makes a moving case for Fanny's never getting over her mistreatment of her sister, culminating in her not being present when Camilla's baby boy was born. The path of self-destructive behavior on which Fanny set herself shortly thereafter lasted for the twenty years she outlived Camilla. Haunted by her sense of having failed her sister, Fanny was unable to carry on her brilliant career after Camilla's tragic death, most likely in Fanny's arms. The fact that she let herself go physically and mentally gives the lie to any pat theory of her as the cold manipulating sister turning her adoring sibling into nothing more than a "wife." Whatever her motives, once she had to acknowledge that she abandoned her dearest tie on earth, she never recovered. The previously witty, articulate, politically astute woman lived out her last years virtually friendless, the victim of nervous breakdowns and unpredictable behaviors.

As Sylvia Strauss clearly argues, Parthenope Nightingale would gladly have fulfilled the ultra-feminine roles in her relationship with her progressive sister, Florence. But unlike Fanny Wright, Florence refused such an alliance. Determined to pursue her career as a humanitarian, she steeled herself against her sister's fits of despondency and her mother's entreaties not to leave Parthenope until she felt quieter about the departure. This sister-bond was filled with recriminations from Parthenope and rages on Florence's part until late in life when a genuine rapprochement was reached. Once again, we find a relationship between two very dissimilar sisters surviving their destructive moves.

While love predominated over other feelings between Emily and Lavinia Dickinson, it remains nonetheless true, as Adelaide Morris pointedly demonstrates, that the New England poet needed to define her sister as essentially her opposite. In their daily lives, Emily cast off many domestic tasks upon a seemingly willing Vinny, while she herself retired to write. Dickinson extended this division of character traits to her sister-in-law, Susan Gilbert Dickinson. Susan became the embodiment of a muse for Emily, someone capable of inspiring rapture and passionate feeling, someone full of excitement and elan. This somewhat arbitrary triangle worked throughout Emily's life and may well have been a major support for her as an artist writing in a singularly hostile environment.

Virginia Stephen Woolf may be the best example of one sister seeing the other as an expanded self. Though her feelings for Vanessa are finally too complex to yield to any single explanation, in certain ways Virginia lived a fuller life through her unbroken and intensely intimate connection with Vanessa. Shortly after their marriage, Leonard Woolf consulted several psychiatrists until he found one who would confirm his own belief that Virginia would not make a fit mother. Recent research by Roger Poole (*The Unknown Virginia Woolf*) would indicate that this process arose as much from Leonard's distaste for fatherhood as from any honest concern for his new wife's mental health. Wanting children very much, Virginia would go through life feeling incomplete. Vanessa seemed to her the fertile mother, the fulfilled woman, and Virginia lavished great affection upon Vanessa's children. She seems to have been a model parent to her nephews and niece whenever Vanessa left them for the sunnier climes of Italy.

Like Virginia, Christina Rossetti believed that her sister Maria had certain qualities that she herself lacked, qualities having to do with Christian piety and acceptance of one's lot. In both her poetry and prose, as Diane D'Amico shows, Christina praises Maria and recognizes that without her sister's example, her own depression and defiance would have poisoned her work and her life. Moreover, she accepted Maria's remonstrances to be more cheerful and full of faith, living with her sister's memory ever before her for all the years she outlived her. Repeatedly, the poet stipulates that remaining close to her sister throughout her life gave her the balance she required.

The Austen sisters, Jane and Cassandra, lived as closely as did the Rossettis, none of them ever marrying, all of them expressing feelings of completeness with one another. By shifting the lighting sufficiently to allow us to view the story within the story, Sue Lanser illuminates Austen's novels for what they can tell us about sisters. Over and over, the structure is essentially the same: two sisters move through their initiations into upper middle-class English life without losing each other. In fact, Lanser forcefully shows that there is a direct correlation between the kind of husband a woman can attract and the success of her prior relationship with her sister. And since many people who knew them spoke of Jane and Cassandra as being "married," and since they used similar language about themselves, Lanser invites us to see this artistic structure as a reflection of Jane's deepest views about her own life with her beloved sister.

This collection ends with an essay on poems by Denise Levertov and Adrienne Rich that speak about their sisters. Robin Riley Fast argues that working through feelings for their own sisters has contributed to each poet's attitudes toward themselves and women in general. What both women come to is that the depth of shared history can soften particular difficulties in the present, and that her bond with her blood sister is filled with ambiguity caused by simultaneous feelings of sameness and difference.

So I end where I began: Sisters often tempt us to believe we can be one with another human being, even as they convince us that we are different from everyone else no matter how close we may become. Yet the stories found in this volume attest to the primacy of that connection of sister with sister, regardless of the complexity and even mystery lying at its heart.

## 2 Sisters and Comrades: The Common Lives of Grace and Edith Abbott

Lela B. Costin

Edith Abbott

Grace Abbott

Among the many persons attracted to Jane Addam's Hull-House in the first decade of the twentieth century were Grace and Edith Abbott. They had grown up in the 1880s and 1890s (Grace, 1878–1939; Edith, 1876–1957) in a small prairie town on the plains of Nebraska with a distinctive way of life that has since vanished from our society. Hull-House and Chicago provided a setting in which the Abbott sisters could find a creative solution to the restrictive status of women, meet their strong personal needs for work and achievement, launch their careers, and contribute to social reform.

Between the Progressive era and the enactment of social reforms in the 1930s, Grace Abbott was a leader among organized women and a highly influential avant-garde public administrator, best remembered for her dynamic direction of the U.S. Children's Bureau during its "glory days." Edith Abbott, in turn, became a towering figure as a "social investigator," a dauntless advocate for the development of a humane system of social welfare, and the chief architect of a pacesetting model of education for the newly developing profession of social work. Before their careers ended, the Abbott sisters had turned their energies and keen minds to a wide range of social, political, and legal issues — woman suffrage, the rights of women in industry, the evils of child labor, the international traffic in women for purposes of prostitution, the immigrant "problem," tenement housing, delinquency, prison reform, the peace movement, the right of women to safety in childbearing. The Abbotts played a major role in turning "charity work" into a new profession, and when the Great Depression swept the country, the Abbott sisters became strong advocates of the old and the new poor and used their wide influence to help gain adequate measures of emergency relief and lasting programs of social security.

A distinguishing ingredient in the unusual achievements of Grace and Edith Abbott was the way in which their lives and careers were inextricably woven into an effective partnership of ideas and actions that challenged many of the prevailing norms of American society. Their writings reflect their common goals, and their different personality traits and particular competencies made possible an enormously effective division of labor. Edith Abbott was the scholar, Grace the younger sister who took the initiative in translating knowledge into action. Yet the boundaries of their separate roles were flexible and their influence and stimulation reciprocal.

Edith had been the somewhat favored child at home, shyer and more fearful than Grace. A former childhood friend remembered her as "the gentle Edie of our playhouse days."[1] In the course of her long career and her fight to advance social justice, Edith lost all vestiges of fearfulness, and she usually hid the sensitivity of her personality behind a wall of austerity and brusqueness. Grace Abbott had been the more harum-scarum, daring, and unpredictable child. As an adult she once referred to herself as the family "ugly duckling." It was she who learned to negotiate herself through official Washington, to interpret unwelcome facts to congressmen and gain support for her proposals, to function effectively within the urbanity common to international government meetings, and, as the U.S. government's chief delegate at such meetings, to preside with sophisticated formality over the social affairs that accompanied such appointments.

The character that Grace and Edith evidenced came in no small measure from their parents. Their father, Othman A. Abbott, had first come to Nebraska in 1867 and settled in the small prairie town of Grand Island where he established a law practice. Their mother, Elizabeth Griffin Abbott, was a respected high school principal in West Liberty, Iowa, at the time of her marriage. In the finest sense of the term, as an observer noted, the senior Abbotts were "aristocrats of the prairie."[2] During the long years of their life together, Othman and Elizabeth Griffin Abbott held in common basic values that never wavered. They believed in the rights of the individual—to think one's own thoughts, speak one's own mind, to act independently and in nonconforming ways as long as the rights of others were not abridged or the sensibilities of others unnecessarily flaunted. They were each unequivocally opposed to slavery when this was a perilously divisive issue in this country. They shared a conviction that not only men but women had rights and these should be equal, that the potential capabilities of women were as important as men's. They believed that the human mind could solve great problems and if properly trained could enhance life for all people and that men and women had a responsibility to nurture and use that highest gift. Neither was religious in the sense of being a "believer," and they eschewed formal religious organizations. But each was loving, humanitarian, compassionate to those who had met misfortune, and willing to share, whether the need be money, their home, or their counsel.

The relationship between their parents maintained a balance and reliability in the Abbott sisters' lively and intellectually stimulating environment. The Abbott family life was not always easy. In a home where speaking out was encouraged, tensions were sometimes high. Nevertheless, in their home, the Abbott parents were equals. They treated each other with love and respect, even when they openly differed with each other. They saw their children as individuals and accorded them respect as well, their daughters no less than their sons, one of whom was the oldest child while the other was the youngest. Grace and Edith were given freedom and encouragement to be themselves, to go freely about their small town, to question, to think, to express their opinions freely at home and away from home, and to attempt any worthy endeavor even against adversities.

When they first went to Chicago in 1908, both Edith and Grace wanted to do something important and useful. For Edith it was a straightforward love of learning and an overwhelming need for greater knowledge that propelled her to the University of Chicago. For Grace it was boredom and awareness of her own potentiality and the lack of opportunity at home.

Many opportunities awaited the Abbott sisters as they entered the new and exciting world of the University of Chicago and Hull-House. Although they lived most of their adult lives in Chicago and the nation's capital, and their careers took them to cities all over the country and into Europe, Grace and Edith were usually referred to as "the Abbott sisters of Nebraska." Prairie life was distinctive; its impact was profound. Another Nebraska woman of the same generation, Willa Cather, described it this way: "We were talking about what it is like to spend one's childhood in little towns like these, buried in wheat and corn, under stimulating extremes of climate; burning summers when the world lies green and billowy beneath a brilliant sky, when one is fairly stifled in vegetation, in the colour and smell of strong weeds and heavy harvests; blustery winters with little snow, when the whole country is stripped bare and grey as sheet-iron. We agreed that no one who has not grown up in a little prairie town could know anything about it. It was a kind of freemasonry, we said."[3]

The years the Abbott sisters spent at Hull-House were germinal ones for them. Certainly Hull-House had a powerful and impressive list of residents, unsurpassed by any other settlement, and Jane Addams had an unusual ability "to create a sense of unity, a sense of purpose among the residents." Edith Abbott stated the reason simply: "We were held together by the sincere and gracious liberalism of Miss Addams."[4] Like most of the Hull-House residents, the Abbott sisters held great admiration and affection for Jane Addams. She in turn had been quick to recognize their talents and potential. Grace Abbott especially moved swiftly into an easy relationship of trust with her, partly because Grace was open, confident, and outspoken. Edith Abbott was inclined to be somewhat more deferential toward Miss Addams. Jane Addams heartily respected the good judgment of both sisters and trusted them even on issues where she was personally vulnerable.

The Abbott sisters' years together at Hull-House were immensely productive for each, not only in tangible and lasting achievements, but in the shaping and firming of the structure of their lifelong partnership. By the time Grace went to Washington, the character of that partnership had become clearer. The two sisters' interests coincided, having been developed together through a close association that began in early childhood.

As the scholar, Edith was always thirsting to establish the facts and a fuller understanding that would provide a more exact base of knowledge for their common endeavors. Her early investigation into women in industry, child labor, tenement housing, the juvenile court, truancy and school attendance policies—all this and more became part of Grace's repertoire of knowledge, on which she relied in the arena of social reform and public administration. She could masterfully interpret data to influential groups whose support was essential to the Abbott sisters' goals. As Edith put it, "I could assemble the facts and write a report, but Grace had the gift of applying the proper legislative remedy"—a statement that, though accurate, reflected Edith's practice in her later years of underplaying her achievements in comparison to those of her younger sister.

In fact, their influence and stimulation were reciprocal, an aspect of their partnership that is apparent from examining their published writings on immigration. Certain leading ideas run through each work, making them seem almost one. These major points of view are ones that Grace Abbott drew out of her daily work with the Immigrants' Protective League and set forth in her annual reports to her board, in her book *The Immigrant and the Community*, and in her report to the Massachusetts Commission on Immigration. In turn, Edith was prompted to begin a long period of research that produced two classic volumes on immigration: *In Immigration: Selected Documents and Case Records* and *Historical Aspects of the Immigration Problem*. In these books she made use of case records (which Grace selected for her from the files of the Immigrants' Protective League) and public documents to which she added her own insightful introductions and interpretations. The result was a sound historical, legal, and philosophic base for the resolution of immigration policy issues that is still of interest today.[5]

As can be seen from their letters to each other, the sisters understood and trusted one another implicitly, never making major decisions without consultation. Each could accurately predict the other's reactions to a new situation, although when it was politic to do so, either one might convincingly convey the impression that she had "no idea what my sister would say." Each worked tremendously hard, Edith more intensely without the relief that might have spared her serious headaches and other forms of stress. Each had a quick wit, but Edith's often had a biting edge, while Grace's was of the kind that cleared the air in any discussion, cut through any person's self-assumed importance, and brought about a more relaxed perspective on the question at hand—even as she bore in with a reminder of the data and a proposed line of action.

As Grace Abbott prepared to leave for the nation's capital to administer the federal child labor law, the sisters' unusual partnership was yet to show the full fruition of their uncommon talents.

The most productive and the final years of the Abbott sisters' partnership occurred in the 1930s. By then each was firmly established in her work—Grace as Chief of the U.S. Children's Bureau and Edith as Dean of the University of Chicago's School of Social Service Administration. The late years of the Hoover administration and the emergence of the New Deal provided an arena in which the Abbott sisters acted as nationally recognized advocates for the old and new poor who endured distress and destitution in the Great Depression. They astutely collaborated to gain fullest use of the resources each brought to their partnership. Edith's long years of scholarship had given her vast knowledge of the antiquated public relief system and the limits of private philanthropy. Her editorial control over an influential social service journal made it possible for the Abbotts to get prompt public attention to their views, fully laid out. Access to the *Social Service Review* allowed Grace Abbott to channel information to her sister from the Washington scene, and, writing under her sister's name, to take positions that she could not state publicly as a member of the presidential administration. In addition Grace brought to the partnership the influence of her political following, her access to government and other national leaders, and the facts she uncovered from Children's Bureau studies of the effects of the Depression on children, families, transient boys, and other special groups.

It has not been possible to clearly define which sister originated the many ideas and undertakings central to their partnership. Both were far ahead of their times in conceptualizing and endorsing social programs to reduce the hazards of life. Sometimes they worked in tandem, but mostly they seemed to be moving along abreast of each other. Both were daring in the way they seized opportunities and accepted risks. Each was assertive and provided forceful leadership in whatever program or movement they became involved in. Each was sometimes termed "dominating," a correct observation if taken to mean that she was confident of her facts and judgments and intent upon making her point of view prevail.

Edith was a more intense personality than Grace. She felt injustice in a personal way, a quality discernible in her writing, which earned for her a title first applied to Florence Nightingale — "passionate statistician."[6] Both sisters worked long hours at office and home, but Edith worked under more stress. In what her father termed "your workshop of a home,"[7] she often sat propped up in bed poring over piles of books and papers about her. Grace was more flexible, more able to remain objective and find a way around difficulties, more able to relax from work by attending a play or a concert or going to a good restaurant with good company, all diversions that Edith enjoyed with her when she came to Washington or they met in New York, but not ones she often sought for herself. Outside her work environment, Edith was not particularly comfortable. She avoided social situations unless they were tied to work in some way and usually hid the softness in her personality. Grace, on the other hand, gave small dinner parties for congenial friends, where their common legislative goals might be discussed for hours but without the intensity that Edith would have brought to the exchange.

Grace sometimes seemed amused by her sister's singular or eccentric ways. In other instances, however, she would try to temper Edith's approach or gently reprove her. When she sent Edith an article critical of the American Red Cross to publish in the *Social Service Review*, she wrote, "I don't care how you cut it up. I think though it will be more convincing if you don't bring in all the heavy artillery you can locate for the attack."[8] By no means was Edith Abbott always austere. When the pressures she felt were somewhat lessened, her manner with students and friends was often considerate, even charming. Often after an argumentative encounter, Edith realized she might have offended and would try to make amends, but not at the expense of softening her convictions.

The Abbott sisters' partnership allowed them to use the resources of government and higher education to get the most out of each. Edith supplied carefully selected personnel for the Children's Bureau from among her more promising students. Grace in turn frequently made student financial aid available to Edith by contracting with her for research to be carried out under Children's Bureau sponsorship and Edith's research direction. If Edith had concluded an investigation that merited wide circulation, Grace might arrange to purchase it from the University of Chicago and publish it in Washington. A promising exploratory study by one of Edith's students sometimes provided the basis for Children's Bureau staff to embark upon a larger piece of research.

In her speeches and in the pages of the *Social Service Review*, Edith Abbott articulated points of view that Grace as chief of the Children's Bureau felt she could not say publicly. Edith might sign such commentary or publish it without signature. "You may think this is too hot to use," Grace once wrote Edith with an enclosed draft of a manuscript, [but] "these things need to be said!"[9] Edith and Grace each read the other's manuscripts and discussed them at length to the end that the final publication sometimes seemed to be as much the work of one as the other. The annual reports of the chief of the Children's Bureau were the work of Grace Abbott and her staff, but Edith's finer editorial hand can sometimes be discerned. Occasional sentences appear that could only be Edith's, as in a discussion of the labor of farm children in North and South Dakota: "The wild geese racing southward at the close of the Indian summer cheer the cold and lonely children as they go round and round the field, counting the days until the ground freezes too deep for plowing."[10] Eight years before it was completed and published, Edith had proposed the idea for Grace's classic work, *The Child and the State*, and had suggested a division of labor.[11] Although the introductions to each of the sections of documents in the volumes clearly reflect Grace's wide experience and points of view, the completed work represented many hours of research, discussion, and writing by each.

Studying the record of the Abbott sisters' activity during the 1920s and

1930s leaves an impression of year after year of crowded schedules, hastily arranged meetings in train stations as their paths crossed in travel, one book after another that had impressed one sister being mailed for the other to read, and letters, telegrams, and manuscripts speeding back and forth between them.

By 1934 Grace was fairly certain that she was ready to resign as Chief of the Children's Bureau, after thirteen demanding years, and join her sister's faculty at The University of Chicago's School of Social Service Administration. Her formal resignation brought an outpouring of commendation for her long service and regret for her departure. Many people shared Eleanor Roosevelt's sentiments: "For so long I have thought of you as a tower of strength in the Children's Bureau that I can hardly bear to think of anybody else trying to take your place."[12] After Grace returned to Chicago, the two sisters lived comfortably together in a large house on Woodlawn Avenue convenient to their work.

The companionable years of the Abbott sisters' maturity were from the outset clouded by intervals of concern over Grace's health. Given earlier serious bouts with tuberculosis, she watched carefully any signs of excessive fatigue or lingering colds. In turn, her physicians tended to study any new symptoms for their relationship to her history of lung disease. Family correspondence from the summer of 1935 on contains increasingly frequent references to Grace's health. By the fall of 1937 she acknowledged an illness that was "not lungs this time."[13]

In April of the following year, Grace Abbott entered a hospital in Chicago for a series of tests of bone marrow. Dr. Martha Eliot, an old friend and fellow member of the Children's Bureau, came to be with her. When the tests were completed, Abbott asked her friend to "go to the laboratory and see what they found and then come tell me." The diagnosis was multiple myeloma. Grace Abbott accepted the diagnosis and its implications stoically. Although she and Dr. Eliot were together a number of times in the months to come, Eliot stated that they never discussed the ultimate consequences of her illness again. It was different for Edith. She was heartbroken. Grace asked Eliot to try to explain her illness to Edith, to help her understand and accept it. Eliot felt she was unsuccessful in her attempt. At the first indication of a terminal illness for her sister, Edith could feel only despair. Cancer then was such a dread disease that it was spoken of only in very guarded circles. Edith insisted that no one be told the nature of her sister's illness. So successful was she in concealing the diagnosis that the literature of the time of Grace Abbott's death and after refers only vaguely to "anemia." More than two decades later, inquires of Abbott's former colleagues and students yielded no reliable information about the nature or duration of her illness.[14]

The shadows darkened rapidly for Grace Abbott in early 1939 and she entered the hospital where she was except for brief intervals until her death in June. Notices of her death at sixty years and accounts of her achievements appeared in newspapers across the country. Telegrams and letters of condolence and admiration for Grace's years of work in the public good poured in, mostly directed to Edith. They came from the President of the United States, senators, and other public officials, jurists, and many other citizens of all walks of life who had known her work and had felt touched by it. Perhaps no accolade came closer to defining her particular genius than that given by Felix Frankfurter: "I do not believe that American experience would disclose a finer illustration of the rare art of public administration. I do not mean to minimize the triumphs of . . . mechanical inventions, but social inventions apparently entail much subtler gifts. . . . The manner in which Grace Abbott translated the blueprints of social policies into effective operating institutions for the benefit of society at large made her work, in every true sense of the phrase, that of social invention."[15]

The days and nights following Grace Abbott's death were harsh ones for her sister. For some months she sought surcease through extensive recollections of her sister's work and achievements and of their childhood together. She wrote carefully designed answers to every expression of sympathy. She became possessive of her sister's personal effects and for a long time would allow nothing to be changed in her sister's room. Always she strived to keep her sister's presence alive in the minds and hearts of others. For some years she sent flowers or a telegram to Martha Eliot on Grace's birthday. Any recognition of Grace was intensely meaningful to her sister, particularly those that fixed Grace's name to a cause—to scholarships, a children's home in South Dakota, a housing division near Hull-House, and a children's hospital wing. Edith Abbott derived special pleasure when a Liberty Ship was named the S. S. *Grace Abbott* in October of 1942. With friends and family she attended the christening ceremony in the Bethlehem Fairfield Shipyards in Baltimore.[16]

The primary effort to bring her grief under control was made through the use of her tremendous capacity for work. Edith's lifelong pattern of concentration and steady movement toward goals held her fast. Nevertheless, some believed that her work was significantly affected by her sister's death. It was said that she had no one to pull her back into reality, no political action outlet for her ideas. It was as though a dam had been put over the river.

Edith Abbott retired as dean in 1942, after eighteen years in that demanding post. Her final professional triumph was her acceptance speech when she was given the Survey Award at the 1951 National Conference of Social Work. The bronze plaque noted her "imaginative and constructive contributions to social work." The conference had been largely devoid of calls for social action, and the slight, frail seventy-five-year-old woman who came to the podium "startled and delighted the large general session audience by turning her acceptance speech into a strong-voiced demand that something be done to abolish the means test and to establish children's allowances."[17]

To those who had known Edith Abbott well, her presence continued to hold them. Between trains in Chicago, Dorothy Bradbury (a former Children's Bureau staff member) once telephoned Edith Abbott, who prevailed upon her to change her ticket so that she could take a few hours and spend them with her at Hull-House, where she had returned to live. Later that night, Edith insisted upon walking to the corner with Bradbury because, she said, the neighborhood was getting dangerous. Looking back at Abbott under the street lamp, it occurred to Bradbury that she was unlikely to see Edith again, and as the taxi drove away she wept at the realization.

The days at Hull-House grew harder for Edith. Glaucoma clouded her vision and made reading and mobility difficult. The weight of the past and unresolved sorrows led her to turn to her father's old remedy for ills, a glass of wine. When it became evident she could no longer live alone, she returned to Nebraska, as she had always expected to.

A beautiful passage in Edith Abbott's writing is a description of her heritage and childhood home: "Grace and I often talked over the vivid memories which we shared of the pioneer days in our part of the Great Plains. . . . And we used to say that if we lived in Chicago a hundred years, we could never forget the call of the meadow larks along the roadside; the rustling of the wind in the corn; the slow flight of the sand-hill cranes over the prairie creek near our home; and the old Overland Trail, a mile from the main street of our town — where the wild plums were hidden and the bittersweet berries hung from the cottonwoods in the early fall."[18]

But these were her memories, and the Nebraska she returned to was a new environment. The old family home had been converted into three apartments. Her brothers, Arthur and Othman Jr., each occupied one of them, and Edith Abbott moved into the third. They lived independently of each other, but with old loves and old rivalries renewed. Edith Abbott was lonely despite her younger brother's close attention. She complained that no one came to see her, that neighbors were afraid of her. Her glaucoma worsened, her body weakened, and her spirit diminished.

On July 22, 1957, Arthur Abbott telegraphed his niece that "Edith is down in bed now and I do not believe she will get out of it." A week later he sent a message that "Edith Abbott died without pain tonight."[19] It had been hard to think of Edith in a weakened condition. As one of Edith's former faculty members wrote, "but perhaps it was a relief to her indomitable spirit to lay aside the burden of a body that no longer served her."[20] The last years of Edith Abbott's life had not been happy ones. Since her cherished values and goals were ahead of her time, they were not particularly conducive to happiness. But with her fighting spirit, she did not consider happiness the object of her life. Her life partnership with her sister, the legacy she left her profession, and the work that earned her the tribute "the noblest Roman of them all in public welfare."[21] — that had been enough.

The record of the Abbott sisters' lives makes evident an effective blending of cherished values and individual competencies turned to the pursuit of social justice. Devoted to each other, drawing strength from their common life, each sister still maintained her own distinct personality, thus enriching the remarkable partnership for which they are remembered.

## NOTES

1. Arnold C. Koenig to Edith Abbott, July 3, 1940. Abbott Papers, Charlotte Abbott Addenda. (Regenstein Library, University of Chicago).
2. Interview with James Brown IV, July 14, 1976.
3. Willa Cather, *My Antonia* (Boston: Houghton-Mifflin, 1918; reprint ed., Riverside Press, 1926), p. ix.
4. Allen F. Davis, *American Heroine. The Life and Legend of Jane Addams* (New York: Oxford University Press, 1973), pp. 117–18; Edith Abbott, Notes and manuscript, Abbott Papers.
5. Grace Abbott, *The Immigrant and the Community* (New York: 1917; Commonwealth of Massachusetts), *Report of the Commission on Immigration. The Problem of Immigration in Massachusetts*, House Report no. 2300 (Boston: Wright and Potter Printing Co., 1914); Edith Abbott, *Immigration: Selected Documents and Case Records* (Chicago: University of Chicago Press, 1924); E. Abbott, *Historical Aspects of the Immigration Problem* (Chicago: University of Chicago Press, 1926).
6. *The Nation*, Jan. 23, 1924, p. 77.
7. O. A. Abbott to Edith Abbott, Mar. 5, 1924, Abbott Papers, C. A. Addenda.
8. Grace Abbott to Edith Abbott, Mar. 2, no year. Abbott Papers, C. A. Addenda.
9. Grace Abbott to Edith Abbott, n.d., Abbott Papers, C. A. Addenda.
10. Children's Bureau, *Annual Report*, 1922, p. 22.
11. Edith Abbott to Grace Abbott, Nov. 24, 1930, Abbott Papers, Box 2, Folder 13; Grace Abbott, *The Child and the State*, Vols. I and II. (Chicago: University of Chicago Press, 1938).
12. Eleanor Roosevelt to Grace Abbott, June 13, 1934, Abbott Papers, C. A. Addenda.
13. Grace Abbott to Elizabeth Shirley Enochs, Sept. 25, 1937, copy of letter supplied by E. Enochs.
14. Interview with Martha Eliot, July 1, 1973; Winifred Walsh "Grace Abbott and Social Action, 1934–39" (Ph.D. dissertation, University of Chicago, 1965), p. v.
15. Felix Frankfurter, "Grace Abbott: Social Inventor," *The Child* 4 (August 1939): 49.
16. Invitation to Edith Abbott from Bethlehem Fairfield Shipyards, Inc. and the U.S. Maritime Commission to attend the launching of the S. S. *Grace Abbott*, on Oct. 10, at 11:30 a.m., Abbott Papers, C. A. Addenda.
17. "A Report of the 78th National Conference of Social Work," *The Survey* 87 (June 1951): 278.
18. Edith Abbott, "A Sister's Memories," *Social Service Review* 13 (September 1939): 352–353.
19. Arthur G. Abbott to Charlotte Abbott, July 22, and July 28, 1957, Abbott Papers, C. A. Addenda.
20. Wayne McMillen to A. G. Abbott, Aug. 1, 1957, Abbott Papers, C. A. Addenda.
21. "1930-Twentieth Anniversary – 1950, The Anniversary Dinner," *Public Welfare* 9 (January 1951): 4.

# 3 Maria: Christina Rossetti's Irreplaceable Sister and Friend

Diane D'Amico

Christina Rossetti

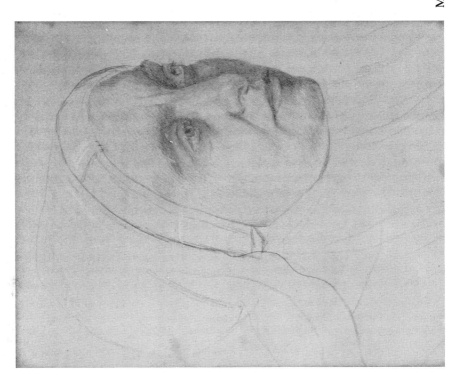

Maria Rossetti

Biographers of Christina Rossetti have tended to see her relationship with her sister Maria in negative terms, suggesting that Maria restrained and stifled Christina's more passionate and imaginative nature.[1] Such a tendency is understandable, for as Christina Rossetti matured, she did become more scrupulous in her behavior, turning more and more to the promises of her faith as solace for hopes deferred. A close relationship with the older Maria, who was at times a bit extreme in her adherence to church doctrine, seems at least in part responsible. However, such a conclusion is itself too restraining, excluding the value of a sister's love, given and received. According to Dante Gabriel Rossetti, in childhood Christina "simply worshipped" Maria.[2] Years after Maria's death, Christina still referred to her as "my irreplaceable sister and friend."[3]

Christina was 46 when Maria died. For all but a few years when Maria was a governess and later when she entered the All Saints' Sisterhood, an Anglican religious order, they lived in the same household, encouraging each other's plans and hopes. When Christina first began writing poetry at the early age of eleven, Maria copied out the finished versions for her, since Maria's penmanship was considered the finer. When Maria had plans for an Italian exercise book, Christina helped her with some of the "subordinate work," desiring to see her sister's name in print, since she and her two brothers had already achieved that success. Most importantly, both Maria and Christina were devout members of the Church of England. (Neither brother shared such religious fervor.) Christina's religious beliefs were inextricably woven into her love and admiration for her sister. To Christina, Maria was one of the most saintly persons she had ever known: Maria was always patient and self-restrained; she showed a willing acceptance of duty and place, and at the end of her life she was able to face death "almost with rapture, for to her the promises of religion were the most assured certainties."[4] For Christina, who often found limits burdensome and was not confident that she would be among the chosen on the last day, Maria was a guiding figure to whom she turned for reassurance. In *Time Flies*, Christina's devotional reading diary, she refers to a discussion she and Maria had about funerals, and we see that her sister's cheerful faith encouraged Christina to hope: "One of the dearest and most saintly persons I ever knew saw nothing attractive in the 'hood and hatband' style towards which I evinced some old-fashioned leaning. 'Why make everything as hopeless looking as possible?' she argued." Christina then adds that while at her sister's funeral, "the November day brightened, and the sun

25

(I vividly remember) made a miniature rainbow in my eyelashes. I have often thought of that rainbow since."[5]

In her prose works, Christina reverently recalls what Maria had said and done, offering such reminiscences so that others might learn as she had from her sister's holy example. Twice (once in a letter and once in *Time Flies*) Christina writes of Maria's refusal to enter the Mummy Room of the British Museum: "I well remember how one no longer present with us, but to whom I cease not to look up, shrank from entering the Mummy Room at the British Museum under a vivid realisation of how the general resurrection might occur even as one stood among those solemn corpses turned into a sight for sightseers" (*Time Flies*, p. 128). Christina offers this anecdote in a most serious tone; she did not see it as a fanciful notion or as in any way overscrupulous. Although we, of course, cannot know exactly what passed through Maria's mind on this occasion, we can gain a better understanding of Christina's high regard for her sister's actions if we examine the context in which she chooses to place this account.

In *Time Flies*, this recollection is given as part of the entry for July 4th, the Feast of the Translation of St. Martin. Christina begins her entry with a brief discussion of this feast day, and while she trusts that St. Martin was exhumed "for honourable enshrinement," overall she believes it is far better to leave the dead at peace in their graves. As a conclusion, she mentions Maria and her regard for the sanctity of the Egyptian mummies. Christina's second mention of this incident can be found in a similar context. Upon returning from Egypt, an acquaintance of William Rossetti's offered him a mummified relic. William, not knowing what to do with what he himself considered "an abnormal gift," offered it to Christina, and she responded: "Had I a moratory, I might willingly accept the loan of 'head and hand' as a *momento mori*; but, as it is, I could not feel easy at keeping bits of fellow-human creatures as curiosities; my preference would be to give them reverent burial. Long ago Maria suggested how awful it would be to be in the Museum Mummy Room on the day of the resurrection."[6] Christina saw her sister's response as a proper respect for the dead, a respect she shared.

Another episode involves Maria's strict following of the Second Commandment and is recorded by Christina as her entry in *Time Flies* for April 15th. This is not designated as any particular feast day; thus she simply places an account of Maria's actions as reason enough for meditation:

> I have never forgotten the courageous reverence with which one to whom a friend was exhibiting prints from the Book of Job, avowed herself afraid to look at a representation which went counter to the Second Commandment and looked not at it.
> A host of us talk "as seeing Him Who is invisible:" she so acted.
> Blessed she who then set to her seal that God is true, and since then has "died in faith." (*Time Flies* , p. 71)

Immediately following this praise of her sister, Christina places one of her own poems, which stresses the necessity of regarding the world to come as the only true one, for all on earth passes away and death is inevitable:

> Oh! What is earth, that we should build
> Our houses here, and seek concealed
> Poor treasure, and add field to field,
> . . . . . . . . . . . . . . . . . .
> While step by step Death nears the door?

Although Maria's actions may still seem to some readers excessive, Christina's praise of such behavior is more understandable if we keep in mind her poem; she simply regarded it as proof of Maria's placing God before all else.

The quality of character Maria displays in both these episodes is self-restraint. To Christina, such a quality was closely aligned to the virtue of patience. Self-restraint was evidence of a patient soul, and a patient soul was a spiritual treasure much to be desired: "Patience is its own reward. It preoccupies the soul with a sort of satisfaction which suppresses insatiable craving, vain endeavor, rebellious desire. It keeps the will steadfast, the mind disengaged, the heart quiet. Patience having little or having nothing yet possesses all things; for through faith and patience the elect inherit the promises."[7] When Christina spoke of herself, there was a marked tendency toward self-deprecation, especially regarding the lack of the calm manner a patient nature would display.

She spoke of herself in relation to her temper when talking to William Sharp about her family. After stressing William's cordial nature, she added, "In fact, I was the ill-tempered one of the family; and my dear sister used to say that she had the good sense, William the good nature, Gabriel the good heart, and I the temper of our much-loved father and mother."[8] William Rossetti adds a note to one of Christina's letters, which indicates that he did not consider her to have ever been ill-tempered with him apart from "mere casual fractiousness in days of quasi-infancy." William Sharp's response to Christina's comment is similar, and it is especially significant for its mention of Maria:

> For myself, I never saw a trace of it [bad-temper], but no doubt this tendency had been subdued long before I knew her. An old friend of hers informs me that she changed completely in this respect after the death of her sister, in 1876, to whom she was passionately attached, and for whose strong and saintly character she had an admiration that was almost extreme. Christina was wont to declare that if Maria had been the younger instead of the elder sister, she would have become famous, but that her home duties and yearly intensifying religious scruples and exercises prevented her.

It is hard to assess how severe Maria was with her younger sister when they were children or whether she ever reprimanded her as harshly as Christina's comment to William Sharp suggests. The reminiscences of brothers and family friends never mention such occurrences. Yet it is clear that Christina believed herself to be bad tempered and that her sister Maria was somehow interwoven in this self-judgment. The key to understanding this may lie in Christina's choice of the word "temper" and how we interpret it. While there is no evidence that Christina was ever unkind or ill-mannered toward others, there is ample evidence in both her prose and poetry that the temper within was not calm:

> When it seems (as sometimes through revulsion of feeling and urgency of Satan it may seem) that our yoke is uneasy and our burden unbearable, because our life is pared down and subdued and repressed to an intolerable level: and so in one moment every instinct of our whole self revolts against our lot, and we loathe this day of quietness and of sitting still, and writhe under a sudden sense of all we have irrecoverably foregone, of the right hand, or foot, or eye cast from us, of the haltingness and maimedness of our entrance (if enter we do at last) into life, — then the Seraphim of Isaiah's vision making music in our memory revive hope in our heart.[9]

In "The Heart Knoweth Its Own Bitterness" (August 27, 1857), the speaker makes it clear that she finds not only this world but those around her woefully inadequate:

> Your vessels are by much too strait:
>   Were I to pour, you could not hold. —
> Bear with me: I must bear to wait,
>   A fountain sealed through heat and cold.
> Bear with me days or months or years:
>   Deep must call deep until the end
> When friend shall no more envy friend
> Nor vex his friend at unawares.[10]

This life offered to Christina Rossetti very little that pleased or fulfilled. Maria's contentment perhaps underscored Christina's inability to accept "the day of quietness" and "hope deferred."

In a study of the relationship between Christina and her sister, one poem that should be considered in some detail is "Goblin Market," probably the most famous, certainly the most commented upon of her works. The poem itself places heavy emphasis on the importance of having a strong sister. Laura, the weaker sister, unable to restrain first her curiosity and then her desire, owes her life and perhaps salvation to the moral strength of her sister, Lizzie. The concluding lines of the poem are in themselves a hymn to sisterhood:

> For there is no friend like a sister
>   In calm or stormy weather;
> To fetch one if one goes astray,
> To lift one if one totters down,
> To strengthen whilst one stands.
>   (*Poetical Works*, p. 8)

Although no dedication is made in the published version of the poem, in the manuscript under the title appears "To M.F.R." And in a copy of an 1893 edition of the *Goblin Market* volume, Rossetti has written beside the poem, "inscribed to my dear and only sister Maria Francesca Rossetti." This marginal note is dated Dec. 7, 1893, which was approximately a year before Christina's death. Clearly, throughout her life, Christina associated this poem with her sister.

The nature of this association has been the topic of interest for Rossetti scholars since Christina's death. William Michael indicated to Christina's first biographer Mackenzie Bell that although he did not "'remember there were at that time [the date at which the poem was written] any personal circumstances of a marked kind,'" he did agree with Bell that "'the lines at the close . . . indicate *something*: apparently C[hristina] considered herself to be chargeable with some sort of spiritual backsliding, against which Maria's influence had been exercised beneficially.'"[11] Some biographers such as Violet Hunt and Lona Mosk Packer have seen in the poem evidence that Maria restrained Christina from becoming sexually involved with a married man.[12] However, no concrete evidence has yet appeared to validate such a reading. Moreover, when looking for biographical clues in poetry, one must be exceedingly cautious. Christina Rossetti was a poet who believed quite firmly in the powers of the poetic imagination: "The Poet Mind," as she called it, could "construct . . . from its own inner consciousness . . . unknown quantities."[13] Therefore, unless further information is discovered concerning Christina's life, we must satisfy ourselves with seeing the poem's connection to Maria in more general terms. Such a connection can be made without undue twisting and turning. In the devotional works, when Christina mentions her sister, she indicates that she owes much to her holy example; so in "Goblin Market" she portrays Lizzie as a woman of model behavior to whom one can turn for strength, especially if one is longing for pleasure beyond the day of quietness and routine.

Lizzie's behavior in the poem, her ability to restrain herself when she hears the goblins crying their list of delicious fruit, is quite similar to Maria's actions regarding the Mummy Room, and in particular the print from the Book of Job: "Lizzie covered up her eyes,/Covered close lest they should look." After Laura gives in to her curiosity, she tells her sister that the fruit looks so delicious that surely it must have come from a "fair" vine. Lizzie thrusts a finger in each ear, shuts her eyes, and runs away. When interpreting the poem's connection to Maria, it is helpful at this point to recall Christina's commentary on the Second Commandment: Anything that harassed through the senses and appealed to a human being's sensual side would prove to be a temptation to break that commandment by leading a person to place some object or some aspect of another human being as "unlike divinity as possible" above

God.[14] Once Laura eats the goblin fruit, that is indeed what happens; she believes the fruit to be "sweeter than honey from the rock." Rossetti has used in this line an allusion to Psalm 81:16, which in the language of Christian symbols is read as a reference to Christ.[15] So completely fooled by her senses is Laura that she believes the fruit will end all sorrow: "Have done with sorrow/I'll bring you plums tomorrow," she cries to her sister. Finally, she becomes so totally absorbed in her desire to satisfy her senses that she is lost in "an absent dream," unable to concentrate on her chores, the daily business of living, and soon she is unable to work at all and unwilling to eat natural food.

Underscoring Laura's fall from grace is Lizzie's continued adherence to the daily routine and the natural order. She does the cleaning, baking, sewing, churning of butter, feeding of poultry, all with "an open heart," "warbling for the mere bright day's delight." She is content, and she accepts the limits placed upon her. When night begins to fall, she knows it is wise to seek the safety of home. And most importantly, she is not lost in her own desires; she loves her sister. Even after Laura eats the fruit, there is no separation; the two still remain "golden head by golden head . . . locked together in one nest." This love combined with the wisdom of her self-restraint enables Lizzie to face the goblins and transform their poisonous fruit into "a fiery antidote" for her sister.

The scene in which Lizzie returns to her sister with goblin pulp and dew upon her face and offers herself to Laura has been much analyzed:

> Eat me, drink me, love me;
> Laura, make much of me;
> For your sake I have braved the glen
> And had to do with goblin merchant men.
> (*Poetical Works*, p. 7)

This scene's Eucharistic allusions and erotic connotations have both been noted; therefore for the purposes of this study, it is perhaps only necessary to point to the significance of the love (which does of course pertain to either erotic or spiritual interpretation), for it is the love that saves.[16] It was love that led Lizzie to undergo her ordeal, and it is Laura's gesture of love for Lizzie that causes her to take the antidote into herself. She embraces and kisses her sister, believing that Lizzie's life must now also be lost for her sake: "Lizzie, Lizzie, have you tasted/For my sake the fruit forbidden?"

In *Time Flies* in her entry for February 17th, Maria's birthday, Christina stresses the need for and power of love:

> One whom I knew intimately and whose memory I revere once in my hearing remarked that unless we love people we cannot understand them. This was a new light to me.
> Another time, after she had taken a decisive step in religion, a friend ap-

pealed to her not to be alienated from her regard: and she answered that goodness wheresoever found she thought she loved more than ever.
  Thus in her lips was the law of kindness.Wisdom rooted in love instructed
her how to give a right answer. (*Time Flies*, p. 34)

Immediately following this remembrance and still within the same entry,
Christina places one of her own poems, which praises love as all in all: "Love
is all happiness, love is all beauty,/Love is the crown of flaxen heads and
hoary,/Love is the only everlasting duty." (*Time Flies*, p. 34)

  The two people who provided Christina with sustaining daily love were
her mother and her sister. In this regard, one further comment should be made
concerning "Goblin Market" and Maria Rossetti. The poem does depict a feminine world of order, duty, and love, which is set against a darker, sinister
world of escapism and indulgence, represented by creatures that are predomi-
nantly masculine. The goblins are referred to as goblin men, as "brother with
queer brother." Moreover, there are no men associated with the world of the
sisters. The only other person mentioned is Jeanie, who apparently did not
have a sister like Lizzie to save her, and although we are told that in later
years Lizzie and Laura marry and have children, Christina includes no direct mention of their husbands. Finally, the lesson Laura teaches these children—the conclusion of the poem, a poem Christina referred to as a "fairy
story"—is not to expect some prince, some strong male figure to appear in
their lives to save them, but to look to a sister to "help one on one's way."

  To suggest that Christina is rejecting the male world completely or por-
traying it as satanic is too extreme a reading and in many ways out of keeping with the rest of her work. However, it is significant that in this, one of
her major poems, she depicts a female-hero. Alone Lizzie has the courage
she needs; there is no father, brother, or lover to whom she turns. When the
circumstances demand, she gathers up her pennies and heads out to face the
goblins. The interest Rossetti shows here in a strong woman able to make
choices is very much in keeping with the rest of her work. Many of Rossetti's early poems reveal her interest in female characters and their love dilemmas found in the novels she had been reading: "Zara" (1847), "Isidora" (1847),
"Nydia" (1848), "Lady Montrevor" (1848). Many of the ballads she wrote during the 1850s and 1860s focus on strong, determined women and the pain of
love: "Cousin Kate," "Maude Clare," "Sister Maude," "Maggie A Lady." Her
convent poems—"The Novice" (1847), "Three Nuns" (1849–50), and "The
Convent Threshold" (1858)—are similar; a woman struggles with the conflicts
love can bring and as a result makes a choice regarding her future life. Although Rossetti wrote comparatively few fictional works, two short stories,
"Maude" (1848) and "Commonplace" (1870), depict a group of women and
the various choices they make. Although a thorough examination of this
theme is well beyond the scope of this present study, such a theme is impor-

tant to at least mention, for it does have relevance to Christina's view of her sister.

Neither Maria nor Christina married. Christina received two marriage proposals, rejecting both ostensibly for religious reasons: James Collinson, proposing when Christina was eighteen, was a Catholic; and Charley Cayley, who proposed when Christina was in her early thirties, was an agnostic. Whether there were other reasons, whether she ever loved either man intensely, whether the sorrow over ill-fated love so often expressed in her poems is in some way related to Collinson or Cayley, all these questions and more have been argued by her biographers. The only point that seems certain is that she did have a lasting affection for Cayley. In any case, the circumstances and the man that would have allowed her to make the sort of marriage she valued and perhaps desired never materialized. In Maria's case, no marriage proposals were ever made. There is some indication that she would have been interested in pursuing a romantic relationship if one had offered itself. She was interested in John Ruskin after he showed her some slight attention, and the painter Charles Allston Collins attracted her interest, but neither relationship developed beyond a brief acquaintance.

Christina made reference to Maria's interest in Ruskin in *Time Flies*. Since the whole entry is relevant to this point on women, love and choice, I shall quote it in full:

> One of the most genuine Christians I ever knew, once took lightly the dying out of a brief acquaintance which had engaged her warm heart, on the ground that such mere tastes and glimpses of congenial intercourse on earth wait for their development in heaven.
> *Then* she knew Whom she trusted: *now* (please God) she knows as she is known.
>
> > Lord, I had chosen another lot,
> > But then I had not chosen well;
> > Thy choice and only Thine is good:
> > No different lot, search heaven and hell,
> > Had blessed me, fully understood;
> > None other, which Thou orderest not.
> > (*Time Flies*, p. 77)

Again we see Christina turning to Maria for guidance, for a model of how one should act regarding the loss of an acquaintance who once engaged the heart. Maria was able to accept what life did or did not offer and to choose contentedly from among the possibilities left her. Her family and her faith were enough, and when she joined the All Saints' Sisterhood she found genuine fulfillment.

Christina's admiration for Maria's choice was all the more marked because of her own realization that she herself could not make such a decision. Despite the fact that Christina was a devout Christian and that her religion was the major force in her life, she often struggled with what she referred to in her autobiographical short story "Maude" as "a sort of desperate wilfulness."[17]

There was a distinct difference between the way the two sisters regarded the very faith that drew them together: "Some believers, perceiving themselves to be undoubted Christians in faith, become serenely or perhaps exuberantly happy in their inner selves: it may be said that Maria Rossetti was of these, for (at any rate in her later years) she felt the firmest confidence of salvation. Not so Christina, who always distrusted herself, and her relation to that standard of Christian duty which she constantly acknowledged and professed" (*Poetical Works*, p. liv).

This is William Michael's assessment, and although he should not necessarily be trusted to have understood everything regarding his sister Christina, on this point her own poetry and prose repeatedly support his view. Christina saw life as a difficult pilgrimage through a dying land:

> There are a hundred subtle stings
> To prick us in our daily walk:
> A young fruit cankered on its stalk,
> A strong bird snared for all his wings,
> A nest that sang but never sings:
> Yea sight and sound and silence stings.
> (*Poetical Works*, p. 343)

Nothing in this life could ever bring fulfillment: "'All the rivers run into the sea; yet the sea is not full.' Man is a still wider sea, a still deeper ocean, a more insatiable abyss: this life and the resources of this life can never fill him."[18] Yet while Christina often longed for the quiet of "dreamless sleep," the waiting time before the resurrection, and for the final consummation promised in heaven, she feared the physical process of death. Most significant of all, Christina feared that after her long, weary pilgrimage she might still fail to be among those chosen citizens of the New Jerusalem.

When Christina turned to her sister in life and then after Maria's death, to her memories, she saw a woman who displayed the very qualities she lacked. Maria was confident in the choices she had made, sure of her faith, and sure of salvation. A poem Christina wrote sometime after her sister's death juxtaposes the sorrow of the speaker over the loss of a beloved friend and the friend's comforting assurance that they shall meet again in heaven. Most likely the beloved friend is Maria:[19]

> My love whose heart is tender said to me,
> "A moon lacks light except her sun befriend her.
> Let us keep tryst in heaven, dear Friend," said she,
> My love whose heart is tender.
> From such a loftiness no words could bend her;
> Yet still she spoke of "us," and spoke as "we,"
> Her hope substantial while my hope grew slender.
>
> Now keeps she tryst beyond earth's utmost sea,
> Wholly at rest tho' storms should toss and rend her,

> And still she keeps my heart and keeps its key,
> My love whose heart is tender.
> *(Poetical Works*, p. 132)

Two other poems similar in tone and subject to this testament to sisterly love are "Safe where I cannot lie yet" and "Our Mothers, lovely women pitiful." (I have simply given the first lines as titles since Rossetti titled neither.) Both of these appeared, along with many other religious poems, in *The Face of the Deep*, Rossetti's last major work. "Safe where I cannot lie yet" serves to complement a brief prayer in which Christina humbly trusts that "some [she] love[s] rest safely in Paradise":

> Safe where I cannot lie yet,
>   Safe where I hope to lie too,
> Safe from the fume and the fret;
>   You, and you,
> Whom I never forget.[20]

"Our Mothers" appears much later in the volume, following a passage concerning the "foolish woman" spoken of in the Book of Proverbs, whose "guests are in the depths of hell." Thus Rossetti's poem honoring mothers and sisters seems to be offered in contrast as an example of the woman whose steps lead to heaven:

> Our mothers, lovely women pitiful;
>   Our Sisters, gracious in their life and death;
>   To us each unforgotten memory saith:
> "Learn as we learned in life's sufficient school,
> Work as we worked in patience of our rule,
>   Walk as we walked much less by sight than faith,
>   Hope as we hope despite our slips and scathes,
> Fearful in joy and confident in dule."
> I know not if they see us or can see:
>   But if they see us in our painful day,
>     How looking back to earth from Paradise
>     Do tears not gather in those loving eyes? —
> Ah, happy eyes! whose tears are wiped away
> Whether or not you bear to look on me.[21]

The longing to join her mother and sister and the present distance between them are underscored by the choice of the word "bear" in the last line and the change of pronoun from first person plural to first person singular. It is as if the sister-speaker, who remains in the "painful day" of earth and time, believes herself far inferior to the gracious and lovely mother and sister in paradise. Again Christina seems to be pointing to her own unworthiness.

When examining the relationship between the sisters, one is apt to wonder if Maria's influence effected Christina's poetic development. Some might be inclined to feel that Maria's scrupulous manner and pious life must have restricted her sister's imaginative powers. However, from the evidence available, it is impossible to draw such a conclusion with any confidence. Certainly it is just as likely that Maria's love and guidance tempered Christina's tones of world-weariness and her grim images of death and despair. For example, the *Later Life* sequence concludes with a description of the "dear unforgotten dead" still watching those on earth, "brimful of love" [for them], and "knowledge" that they will someday impart. It is a comforting image, especially when juxtaposed to the depiction of loss of life and soul so vividly presented by Christina in Sonnet 27 from *Later Life*, in which there is no joy and no salvation. It is as if Maria's own happy life and death helped her sister quiet her lingering fears and doubts. Despite what one might think of Maria's actions and choices — what pictures she did or did not look at, what rooms she did or did not enter — it is clear that to Christina Rossetti she was always her "irreplaceable sister and friend."

## NOTES

1. Edmund Gosse's comments in *Critical Kit-Kats* (New York, Scribner's Sons, 1914 p. 160) early set the tone for this negative assessment of Maria's influence: "The influence of Maria Francesca Rossetti on her sister seemed to be like that of Newton upon Cowper, a species of police surveillance exercised by a hard, convinced mind over a softer and more fanciful one." R. D. Waller in *The Rossetti Family* (Manchester, Manchester University Press, 1932, p. 179) criticizes Gosse on this point; however, there is still a tendency to give more emphasis to the possible negative effects of Maria's influence upon Christina than the positive effects of sisterly love and guidance. In the most recent biography of Christina, *Christina Rossetti: A Divided Life*, Georgina Battiscombe (Holt, Rinehart and Winston, New York, 1981), stresses Maria's narrowing influence: "Clearly Maria's influence can only have strengthened Christina in her obsession with small failings and her overanxious preoccupation with the letter of the law" (p. 161).
2. William Sharp, "Some Reminiscences of Christina Rossetti," *The Atlantic Monthly* 75 (1895): 738.
3. *Family Letters of Christina Georgina Rossetti*, ed. William M. Rossetti (1908; rpt. New York: Haskell House, 1968), p. 152.
4. *Dante Gabriel Rossetti: His Family Letters with A Memoir by William Michael Rossetti* (1895; reprint ed., New York: AMS Press, 1970), I, 346.
5. Christina Rossetti, *Time Flies: A Reading Diary* (London: Society for Promoting Christian Knowledge, 1885), p. 2 — hereafter cited within the text as *Time Flies* with page number. Throughout *Time Flies* Christina does not refer to Maria by name; however, a copy housed at the Humanities Research Center (University of Texas at Austin) contains marginal notes in Christina's hand that give her sister's name when Maria is mentioned in the text. I would like to thank the Humanities Research Center for providing me with photocopies of the appropriate pages. It seems that Maria had a salutory effect upon the whole Rossetti household. When Dante Gabriel Rossetti found that Maria had announced she intended to enter All Saints' Sisterhood, he wrote to his mother, "She will indeed be a great loss, being much the healthiest in mind and cheeriest of us all, except yourself. William comes next, and Christina and I are nowhere." (see *Dante Gabriel Rossetti*, II, 297).
6. *Family Letters of Christina Rossetti*, p. 76.

7. Christina Rossetti, *The Face of the Deep: A Devotional Commentary on the Apocalypse* (London: Society for Promoting Christian Knowledge, 1892), p. 117.

8. Sharp, *Some Reminiscences*, p. 740.

9. Christina Rossetti, *Called to be Saints: The Minor Festivals Devotionally Studied* (London: Society for Promoting Christian Knowledge, 1881), p. 435.

10. *The Poetical Works of Christina Georgina Rossetti with Memoir and Notes*, ed. William Michael Rossetti (London: Macmillan, 1904), p. 192 — hereafter cited in the text as *Poetical Works* with page number.

11. Mackenzie Bell, *Christina Rossetti: A Biographical and Critical Study* (London: Macmillan, 1898), p. 231.

12. Violet Hunt in her biography of Elizabeth Siddal, *Wife of Rossetti* (London: John Lane the Bodley Head, 1932), p. xiii expresses her view that Maria restrained Christina from eloping with James Collinson, who was at the time of Maria's supposed intervention a married man. Lona Mosk Packer in *Christina Rossetti* (Berkeley, California: University of California Press, 1963) maintains that Christina was throughout her life in love with William Bell Scott, also married.

13. *Three Rossettis: Unpublished Letters to and from Dante Gabriel, Christina, and William*, ed. Janet Camp Troxell (Cambridge: Harvard University Press, 1937), p. 143.

14. Christina Rossetti, *Letter and Spirit: Notes on the Commandments* (London: Society for Promoting Christian Knowledge, 1883), pp. 70–71.

15. See Christina Rossetti's *Seek and Find: A Double Series of Short Studies of the Benedicite* (London: Society for Promoting Christian Knowledge, 1879), p. 260 for her interpretation of Psalm 81:16: "Thus not sun and star alone set Him forth: but the rock symbolizes His unfailing strength . . . and is all the more like Him when it yields refreshment . . . or sweetness."

16. Maria Shalkhauser in her article "The Feminine Christ," *Victorian Newsletter*, 10 (1956), 19–20 offers a perceptive discussion of the Christian symbolism throughout the poem. Several works have referred to the sexual connotations. Stephen Prickett's *Victorian Fantasy* (Hassocks, Sesses: Harvester, 1979), pp. 103–106 is one of the most recent.

17. Christina Rossetti, *Maude: Prose and Verse*, ed. R. W. Crump (Hamden, CT: Archon, 1976), p. 54. Christina's entry for April 21 in *Time Flies* is also enlightening on this point: "Once in conversation I happened to lay stress on the virtue of resignation, when the friend I spoke to depreciated resignation in comparison with conformity to the Divine Will . . . If only we — if only I were as *resigned* as he was *conformed!*"

18. Rossetti, *The Face of the Deep*, p. 213.

19. See Bell, *Christina Rossetti*, p. 341: Bell quotes William Michael's response to his inquiry regarding whether or not the poem relates to Maria: "I certainly regard it as applying to Maria. The 2nd line, 'a moon lacks light' is conclusive to me. Maria had a very round face, and Christina was much in the habit of calling her Moon, Moony, etc. I have no doubt that Maria on some occasion made this her cue for saying something very like what appears in the poem. However I never knew her to call C[hristina] her 'Sun,' or anything of that sort."

20. Rossetti, *The Face of the Deep*, p. 205.

21. Rossetti, *The Face of the Deep*, p. 401.

# 4 Of Fanny and Camilla Wright: Their Sisterly Love *

Celia Eckhardt

*The material found in the first two pages of this essay echoes work from the full-scale biography, *Fanny Wright: Rebel in America*. Harvard University Press, Cambridge, MA, 1984.

Camilla Wright

Frances Wright D'Arusmont

Of natural sisterhood, of ties that are irrevocable, I have no experience. As I watch my stepdaughters, born only a year apart, I find myself taken aback by the raw competition they carry into their middle thirties. I worry that they risk too much when they behave so badly to each other, yet I know their bonds are deeper than any I shall ever have. Those bonds are no mere function of the will, nor do they come from an instinct toward kindness: They are part of their "given."

And so when I began to piece together the lives of Frances and Camilla Wright I felt at some disadvantage. I had no feeling for the inextricable mixture of ordinary and intense that those who pass their days together over a period of many years must know. At the same time, the circumstances that bound Fanny and Camilla were by no means usual; the events that drew them together marked them differently; and the forces that destroyed them derived from what had once been their strength.

Of the two, it is only Fanny whom history remembers, for John Stuart Mill properly called her one of the most important women of her day. She was important because she dared to take Thomas Jefferson seriously when he wrote, "All men are created equal," assuming that "men" meant "women" as well. She was important because she made of her life a determined search for a place where she could help forge the institutions that would allow that principle to govern society. She was important because she had the integrity and courage to renounce the upper middle-class world to which she was born — a world whose prizes and comforts were hers for the taking — and to risk her health, her fortune, and her good name to realize the ideals on which America was founded.[1]

In 1825 she became the first woman in America to act publicly to oppose slavery. Twenty miles outside the little trading post in Tennessee so presumptuously named Memphis, she established a commune whose purpose was to discover and then to demonstrate how slaves might be educated and responsibly freed. In 1828 she became the first woman in America to speak in public to a large secular audience of men and women, and the first to argue that women were men's equals and must be granted an equal role in all the business of public life. Along with Robert Owen's eldest son, Robert Dale Owen, she edited a liberal weekly newspaper, the *Free Enquirer*, and from 1828 to 1830 she used its pages, as she used lecture halls throughout the country, to fight for all the victims of the social and political hierarchies of her time.

The pampered daughter of a favored class, Fanny cast her lot with working people and, as speaker and journalist, involved herself in the beginnings of the labor movement in New York. She attacked an economic system that allowed not only slavery in the South but what she called wage slavery in the North, a system that made black women the sexual prey of white men and drove poor women everywhere to the workhouse, to crime, and to prostitution. She came to see what Alexis de Tocqueville did not: that America was by no means a society in which people lived as equals, but one marked by extremes of wealth and poverty that were growing rather than diminishing. She understood that such disparities of wealth made an authentic republic impossible.

Nor did the churches escape her wrath. She showed her skepticism of the religious and sexual pieties of her time when she wrote Mary Wollstonecraft Shelley that men, "like their old progenitor, Father Adam . . . walk about boasting of their wisdom, strength, and sovereignty, while they have not sense so much as to swallow an apple without the aid of an Eve to put it down their throats." She attacked a morality that taught people to spend their money building churches and sending missionaries abroad but that closed their eyes to the destitution and injustice around them. She took on the churches in part because she thought men used religion to keep women foolish, dependent, and at home.[2]

At a time when women's virtue was said to depend on their chastity, she spoke of sexual passion as "the strongest and . . . the noblest of the human passions" and the source of "the best joys of our existence." With the possible exception of Walt Whitman, she wrote more powerfully of sexual experience than any other American in the nineteenth century. In 1827, when propriety forbade women from even mentioning sexuality, she publicly endorsed miscegenation as a way to solve the race problem in America. She looked to the day when "the olive of peace" would be "embraced by the white man and the black, and their children, approached in feeling and education, [would] gradually blend into one their blood and hue."[3]

In the 1840s she came to believe that governments made by men were inclined to war. She was convinced that men did this because they elevated the selfish principle over the generous, in part by restricting women to "the narrowest precincts of the individual family circle . . . by forcibly closing [their] eyes upon the claims of the great human family without that circle." Justice, she argued, could come only when "the two persons in human kind — man and woman — shall exert equal influence in a state of equal independence." She anticipated by ninety years many of the ideas Virginia Woolf expressed even more eloquently in *Three Guineas*.[4]

To be called a Fanny Wrightist in America in the 1830s was no less threatening than being called a communist in the 1950s. No doubt because she was so radical, history has not yet done justice to Fanny Wright. As I suggested above, history has altogether ignored her sister, but without Camilla, Fanny's story would not have been written.

Fanny was born on September 6, 1795, and Camilla on March 3, 1797. They and their older brother Richard were born into an upper middle-class Scottish family of some distinction. But in the spring of 1798 their world collapsed: within two months both their parents died. The three children were then separated and taken from their family home in Dundee, on the southeast coast of Scotland—Fanny to be raised at the far end of the British Isles in London by her maternal grandfather and her eighteen-year-old aunt, Frances Campbell. In neither Fanny's published nor private writings could I find a sense of play or childhood. Camilla was left with foster parents who were kind, and she seems to have been too young to be scarred profoundly by the tragedy of their childhood. However, it proved to be the most terrible thing that ever happened to Fanny Wright.

The sisters were reunited in 1806, when Fanny was eleven, but only after she had learned the hard lessons of childhood solitude. Some five years after their parents' death, their uncle had died in India, leaving a substantial fortune to be divided in two equal portions between his sister Frances on the one hand, and his nieces Fanny and Camilla Wright on the other. Miss Campbell had then moved to Dawlish in Devonshire, where she set up in a style appropriate for raising young women according to the highest standards of decorum in the Jane Austen world in which she found herself. And there Camilla joined her sister, probably in the twenty-room mansion Miss Campbell called "The Cottage," which sat halfway up a hill with a view of Lyme Bay near where the English Channel joins the Atlantic Ocean. Fanny later wrote of being surrounded by "rare and extensive" private libraries, and she commanded governesses and tutors of evident distinction.

The pattern of the sisters' relationship was set early and traces that of the traditional marriage. Fanny was the star and Camilla her faithful reflector. Fanny walked boldly through the world while Camilla kept the house. Fanny talked, and Camilla listened. In the autobiography she wrote many years later, Fanny attributed the seriousness of her own character to "the heart solitude of orphanship, to the absence of all sympathy with the views and characters of those among whom her childhood was thrown, [and] to the presence of a sister who looked to her for guidance, and leaned upon her for support."[5]

Even their bodies seemed to reflect their relative power. Fanny was very tall by the time she was fourteen, and when full grown she was at least five feet ten inches, and possibly six feet tall. Washington Irving would call her a tall, thin, talking woman, and the fact that she was so conspicuous was central to her life. Camilla's height, on the other hand, was sufficiently ordinary that no one remarked on it. While Fanny described herself as more like Minerva than Venus, Robert Dale Owen would say she looked rather like a Mercury, and critics often called her masculine. Camilla, however, was soft and easier to miss. The only picture of her that remains is not an authentic portrait, but rather a drawing done by a spiritual medium some half century after she died and identified by Robert Dale Owen as an idealized version of her. She strikes me there as demure and self-effacing, though I inevitably bring to this strange picture the sense of her I get from their letters and the letters of their friends, along with the lineaments of her life. She committed herself to her dazzling older sister when she was very young, and life for her became unthinkable apart from Fanny. This commitment would provide the extraordinary drama she lived out to the far boundaries of personal tragedy.

Their adolescence was a mixture of convention and rebellion, and aside from their own tightening bonds, its central emotional fact was that Fanny hated their aunt. Her reasons for this corroding hatred remain obscure. Everything about Frances Campbell suggests a woman of the utmost propriety. She was apparently good company, since her wealthiest neighbors, Sir Charles Hoare and his wife, asked her some years later to live with them in Luscombe Castle, and she did so for many years. One young man described her as fussy and said she kept after him with "advices" he clearly found ludicrous and oppressive. Nothing remains to indicate Camilla's sense of her. But whether Fanny's hatred derived from real child abuse, as she implied, or was the fruit of her projected anger at her parents' loss, it was no ordinary passion. It directed the course of her future, as Fanny shaped her own character in rebellion against the Tory world Miss Campbell embodied. She saw that the wealthy landowners of Dawlish, who were Miss Campbell's friends, drove the poor contemptuously from their land, and she resolved to be a champion of the humble. She used her extraordinary intelligence and an education more rigorous than that available even to most of the men who were her peers and turned it eventually against her own class.

The Wright sisters left their Devonshire adolescence and their aunt's tutelage with all the graces and promise of the British gentry. Their uncle, James Mylne, wrote of them that they were "girls of whom I may be justly vain — well-principled, well-informed, elegantly accomplished, fit to take their places among society of any rank and to be received in it with esteem and respect." Had she been left to her own devices, Camilla would doubtless have become both a responsible member and an ornament of the society into which she had been born. Her commitment to her sister, however, made a settled life impossible. Fanny's formidable will registered its first major victory when she took Camilla and left Dawlish before even *she* was legally of an age to go. And such was Camilla's loyalty that we have no reason to believe she left that comfortable, gracious world with regret.[6]

Sometime in 1813 or 1814 they went to Glasgow to live with their paternal great-uncle, James Mylne, his wife, their Aunt Agnes, and the five Mylne children. Mylne was Professor of Moral Philosophy at the University of Glasgow, a chair Adam Smith had held forty years before. Though the family lived in a cramped university house, they found abundant compensation for its inconveniences in the vitality of the intellectual life they shared with his colleagues and their friends. Some years earlier Frederick Lamb had written of this circle that the ladies were "contaminated with an itch for philosophy and learning" and had, it seemed, a wonderful time: "After cheese they hand around the table a bottle of whisky and another of brandy, and the whole company, males and females . . . indulge in a dram. It is very comfortable and exhilarating, and affords an opportunity for many jokes." For a group that met regularly to discuss literature and ideas, Fanny wrote a series of plays, along with a treatise on Epicurean philosophy that she later published under the title *A Few Days in Athens*. She clearly established herself there as a promising writer and intellectual. Her great-aunt, Elizabeth Robinson Montagu, had been the first of the blue-stockings — Samuel Johnson had fondly called her "Queen of the Blues" — and Fanny seemed to be taking after her. One admirer wrote that Fanny would soon have the world at her feet. Camilla, on the other hand, she expected to make the perfect wife.[7]

But Camilla found no suitor as interesting and compelling as her sister. Although Fanny indulged briefly in romance with a young man whose character was solid but who seems finally to have bored her, during these years when Camilla was most eligible she left no record of attachment to anyone but Fanny. She followed her in exploring the Highlands in the summers and led the others in applause when Fanny read her latest composition. And when Fanny grew restive, Camilla was ready to pack her bags and go.

In a day when travel was exhausting, bruising, and often dangerous, Fanny's restlessness took them to places even men of their class were unlikely to visit. In 1818 they sailed from Liverpool for New York — Fanny determined to study republican ideals in practice. If seasickness could be taken as a measure of the price Camilla paid in attending on her sister, that cost would have to be ranked very high indeed; for Camilla's suffering was so unrelieved during that first thirty-day voyage that she developed a horror of the ocean trip that never abated. Fanny, on the other hand, was chillingly matter-of-fact: "Take pills regularly while at sea," she later wrote a friend: "Be on deck as soon and as much as possible and above all keep yr bowels open . . . For the first two or three days after every attack of retching drink gruel or water . . . As the appetite comes eat moderately and drink still more moderately. Pills of rhubarb and aloes mixed are as good as any." Among the first travelers to make the journey for what they called pleasure, they sailed up the Hudson and crossed the Mohawk River Valley, finding their way to Niagara Falls and then along the lakes into Canada. They went south from New York to New Jersey, Pennsylvania, and Maryland and finally to the infant capital of Washington, D.C. Together they collected impressions that Fanny would work into a book with which she hoped to capture the attention of some of the most important people of their day.[8]

By the time they were in their middle twenties, it was clear that Fanny and Camilla were crucial to each other. On the simplest level, each provided the other with a badge of respectability at a time when proper women did not live or travel alone. They obviously enjoyed each other's company, and a New York acquaintance wrote that their sisterly love was very beautiful. If Fanny gave Camilla a world far more spacious than she would have found alone, Camilla's role was equally important in her sister's life: she gave her the devotion that undergirded the psychic strength Fanny needed to break one taboo after another. While others advised Fanny to stop or counseled caution, Camilla endorsed whatever it was she wanted to do. As Fanny gradually discarded the anonymity that proper society demanded of women, Camilla stood by, giving her permission, her love, and her expectation that her sister would be great. For the richness of her sister's gifts to her, Camilla was profoundly grateful. Fanny took Camilla largely for granted.

Fanny's book, *Views of Society and Manners in America*, was published in 1821 to Tory attack and Republican praise, and Camilla had to learn to live with less of her sister's attention. They went to Paris to share rooms in an old convent with a family they had met in America, whose youngest daughters, Julia and Harriet Garnett, had become their closest friends. Here Fanny was captivated by the Marquis de Lafayette, who lavishly admired her book and became her mentor. For the next three years the Wright sisters, singly or together, went back and forth between Paris and Lafayette's chateau, LaGrange, forty miles outside the French capital. Fanny became a familiar in Republican salons that were demanding schools in wit and elegance, and Camilla, along with Julia and Harriet, served as her chaperones. Contemptuous of gossip, however, Fanny saw Lafayette on occasion alone. Old enough to be her grandfather but notorious for his interest in pretty young women, Lafayette accepted her devotion with the grand seigneur's appetite for worship. It should have come as no surprise that scandalous rumors began in the spring of 1824, suggesting that Fanny was his mistress and exercised undue influence over him. Lafayette's family, who had gradually chilled to them, now turned decidedly against the Wrights, insisting, among other things, that when he accepted President James Monroe's invitation to come to America in the fall as the Nation's Guest, Fanny and Camilla, if they went at all, should not accompany him on the same ship. Fanny tried to persuade Lafayette to still the gossip by either marrying her or adopting her and Camilla, but Lafayette demurred and the family got their way.

By the fall of 1824 Camilla must have known that loyalty to Fanny would often mean living in opposition to others, and at times could seem defiant of the world's opinion. Lafayette's American tour made this plain. Eleanor Custis Lewis, Martha Washington's granddaughter, conspired with her old friend George Lafayette, who was accompanying his father, to persuade the general not to allow the Wright sisters to travel as part of his entourage. Camilla held true, blaming Lafayette's family for the disappointments she and Fanny suffered at his hands, and deciding she would rather take poison than go back to France with him and take up the life they had led there before.

She learned something further about the physical cost of staying at Fanny's side. After a 600-mile ride on horseback she developed a carbuncle on her back. The doctor said it was the worst he had ever seen and speculated that it was caused by the pressure of her corset bone as they rode relentlessly from Indiana deep into Pennsylvania. Furthermore, Camilla noticed that the heat which seemed to oppress everyone else served to envigorate Fanny. But their trip from New York to New Orleans and then to Boston had so wasted Camilla that she and Fanny finally went to what Thomas Jefferson called "our medicinal springs" to see if she could recover her health.

With no crippling regret, Camilla lent her enthusiasm to Fanny's decision to stay in America. They had met a remarkable man called George Flower, who had emigrated from England a decade before, and together he and Fanny had drawn up a plan for a cooperative colony modeled on a town in Indiana named Harmonie. It had been built in ten years by a German pietistic sect called the Rappites, some of whom were illiterate peasants, and had just been bought by the British industrialist and philanthropist Robert Owen as a place to begin his "new moral world." Imagining a combination of old and new, Fanny and Flower set up their colony outside Memphis, Tennessee, its purpose being to discover and demonstrate how slaves could be responsibly educated and subsequently freed. Camilla believed in the goal and in her sister. Her admiration, in fact, passed all bounds, as she wrote the Garnetts: "I marvel not that all should fall short in comparison with her, for the more I see of life, and above all of womankind, the more I am persuaded her equal never can and never will be found." Their colony, which Fanny named Nashoba, demanded of the Wrights that they leave their class privileges behind to work for long hours with the slaves to clear the land, learning at the same time how to live within the limitations of a system they despised.[9]

After several months at Nashoba, Fanny decided their project was well enough begun, and curious to see what Owen was accomplishing, she left for New Harmony. By now it had come to seem natural that Camilla should keep things going that Fanny started, and she stayed behind. Fanny was exhausted when she returned some weeks later and soon fell seriously ill. Camilla and James Richardson, a Scotsman they had met in Memphis, nursed her day and night. But no sooner had she seemed to recover, than Camilla caught the fever from her. Fanny nursed her and brought on a relapse, and so the exchange went through the fall of 1826.

It was at this point in their lives that I began most bitterly to suffer the biographer's frustrations, because the available evidence is meager, and the consequences of what soon happened proved momentous in Camilla's life, and then in Fanny's. I was bewildered by the fact that George Flower, who had been Fanny's equal partner at Nashoba, left and took his family back to Illinois. For days I arranged the pieces in different patterns, trying to find one that seemed compelling, when suddenly they seemed to arrange themselves. I discovered with surprise that I had come to believe that Fanny had had an affair with Flower and that the affair had become too powerful for Nashoba to contain it. He was married to a very possessive woman, and they had several small children. The strain on him, it seemed, had become intolerable, and he had left. His leaving doomed Nashoba as they had envisioned it, for he was the only person there who had an easy working relationship with black people and experience as a farmer. In her illness Fanny began to shift her attention from slavery and to talk and write about how intolerably crippling marriage was.

Suffering repeated relapses of fever, Fanny decided in the spring of 1827 to go to Europe to try to recover her health. Accustomed by now to doing what Fanny wanted, Camilla agreed to remain at Nashoba. Fanny was convinced that one of them had to be there, and that she herself would die if she stayed much longer. She was of course troubled when she left Camilla, but James Mylne was appalled. He wrote Julia Garnett wondering if Fanny's "excessive passion for notoriety had led to an incipient disorder of the mind." He assumed that Camilla was left there with blacks debased by ignorance and slavery and with whites corrupted by "the absurd principles of [Fanny's] senseless system." He imagined Camilla "dispirited, and broken-hearted by her absence [and facing] all the horrors of a forest solitude."[10]

However she tried to put a good face on it, Fanny had put her sister at serious risk. The inequality at the root of their relationship now bore bitter fruit, and her eight-month absence proved critical in Camilla's life, as well as in her own. For more than twenty years, Camilla had taken whatever direction Fanny set, and now she turned for guidance to others. She allowed James Richardson to send a newspaper called *The Genius of Universal Emancipation*, a log he kept of Nashoba events. In it he announced that Nashoba held "the proper basis of the sexual intercourse to be the unconstrained and unrestrained choice of *both* parties." He said that Camilla Wright had explained this philosophy to the slaves and ended by announcing that he had begun to live there with a quadroon woman called Josephine Prevot. This was a time in America when women could not properly mention sex at all. Free love was unthinkable and miscegenation a crime of the vilest order. People who had been close friends and supporters responded with shock. In the face of a general reaction that Fanny was running a brothel at Nashoba, Camilla proceeded as though nothing untoward had happened.

Assured that Fanny would soon tell the world her own view of marriage as an oppressive institution, Camilla had begun to live with Richardson Whitby, a Shaker who had come to try to take George Flower's place. Shortly before Fanny returned the following January, however, Camilla married Whitby, justifying what seemed a lapse from principle on the grounds that living "in open violation of the civil institutions of the country" provoked widespread indignation. The public outrage over what the *Genius* printed was so intense that Camilla and Richardson had in fact destroyed what was left of Nashoba and branded the Wright sisters for life. It is possible to imagine that Camilla acted as she did in unconscious revenge for being left behind. It is equally possible to imagine that her long-standing dependence made her incapable of acting with full maturity. But it is not possible to know with any certainty why she acted as she did.[11]

For six months after her return from Europe, Fanny held on to Nashoba, but at last she left it to the slaves and an overseer hired to supervise them. But it was Camilla whose future became most precarious through so marked a change in their plans. She had married Whitby when she assumed that her life and Fanny's would be spent either in the backwoods of Tennessee or at Robert Owen's New Harmony. Now both experiments in new social living had failed, and Fanny decided to become a public teacher, lecturing and editing with Robert Dale Owen the newspaper they christened the *Free Enquirer*. She wanted to move to a more central location in one of the big eastern cities, but Camilla was pregnant.

No one seems to have thought that Whitby would survive transplanting to an urban setting, and Camilla was faced with choosing between her sister and her husband. She chose Fanny, and announced that after her baby was born in Memphis she would rejoin her sister. As both of them had written stiffly of the marriage and two of their friends referred to Whitby as boorish, her choice may have been less than wrenching. But it would have seemed to put an extra obligation on Fanny which she was not able to acknowledge or perhaps did not feel. She left Camilla in Memphis to bear the terrors and dangers of childbirth without her and started out on her mission to transform America.

The delivery proved difficult, and the doctor at best incompetent. In the fashion of the day, he bled Camilla repeatedly, though she had already lost a good deal of blood, and he gave her a purgative she said must have had a noxious element in it as it nearly killed her. The baby was a boy, and she named him Francis. When Fanny got Camilla's letter telling what had happened, she was obviously shaken. Writing that she'd have come if she could, she said nevertheless that the country was politically aroused: "Were I but free I should fly to you, lamb. But to leave were impossible." The self-confidence so crucial to the extraordinary woman she had become had hardened into a self-importance that blinded her even to her sister's need. A comment Camilla made in a letter to the Garnetts suggests that her suffering was by no means merely physical.[12]

Four months later Camilla left her husband. She made the trip as far as Cincinnati with a friend from Memphis, but the rest she managed with the baby alone. In New York she took up the responsibilities of housekeeper in the mansion Fanny had rented for those involved in putting out the *Free Enquirer*. Only a few weeks later her sister left to speak in Boston.

A few days after Fanny got back, Camilla's baby died. Camilla had started a letter to Julia Garnett some two weeks earlier, and she took it up again in a tremulous hand: "Alas! Alas! how shall I paint my bitter sorrow and anguish [sic] my son, my lovely babe, who was playing at my feet while I wrote the above, now sleeps in the cold earth while his wretched and bereaved mother yet lives to bewail her irrecoverable loss." But for Fanny's care she said she would "have been bereft of reason or of life by this stroke so sudden, so severe!" Fanny added in helpless postscript, "It is sad to centre the affections too strongly and closely in beings so fragile yet how to help it!"[13]

The life the sisters had shared for more than twenty years had already begun to disintegrate, and now Fanny pursued her causes as Camilla sank gradually into irreversible despair. We know nothing about how this happened, or what was said between them. But only two months after the baby died, Fanny left Camilla in New York to make the trip to Haiti to free the slaves she had bought in Tennessee. In her absence Camilla wrote Harriet Garnett: "the sister — the friend with whom from my earliest childhood I have felt my being identified — for whom I have suffered much and with whom I have sympathized still more is no longer the sharer of my thoughts and feelings and only ceased to be so from my discovering that *I shared not hers*." Camilla felt that she had once taken a place in Fanny's heart but now was minor, "if not altogether lost in the midst of the wide sea whereon she is now embarked."[14]

Camilla was not alone in her self-destructiveness. Despite Fanny's commitment to public life and her deep belief that she had a crucial role to play in America, she now undermined herself. As though perversely to make up for what Camilla had lost, she returned from Haiti pregnant by a man many other people despised, William Phiquepal d'Arustmont. She had written earlier about how brutal society was to a child it called illegitimate and had said that sexual intercourse should be governed by a couple's responsibility to the child they created. Now she apparently saw no alternative to leaving America and marrying. In early July she and Camilla sailed from New York for Europe.

My necessary dependence as a biographer on a few scraps of information had long since grown intolerable, and I consoled myself for the meager facts by imagining what the great Swedish director Ingmar Bergman would do with the fragments I had. I imagined the silences. I imagined, so long as I could bear it, the confusion and the pain. I imagined the sickness that invaded the mind. But I could write of none of this because I simply did not know.

What I knew was that Fanny and Camilla disappeared when they got to France. I knew that Fanny wrote back to the *Free Enquirer* from somewhere in the provinces. I knew that Camilla went south to Bordeaux, possibly alone, though perhaps with friends. And I calculated that Fanny's baby was born in January, 1831, in Camilla's telling absence. The measure of Fanny's suffering could be taken by the fact that when she appeared suddenly at one of Lafayette's soirees, she excited a good deal of attention because she looked terrible. She was snubbed by the women there and did not return. James Fenimore Cooper, who saw her that day, clearly wanted to meet her, but as he thought it would show disrespect to his wife to ask for an introduction, he did not.

Early in February Camilla came back to Paris from the south of France and got an apartment by herself. She died there on the eighth of that month. Rumor had it that she died alone, but Fanny wrote Robert Owen that she had died in her arms "of a sudden attack of hermorrage [sic], after having flattered me with perfect recovery from the weak state of health and spirits wch [sic] had decided me on a voyage to Europe." Nothing for Fanny was ever the same again.[15]

The circumstances of their last year and a half together had made Fanny's loss all the more irreparable. Whatever had happened between them — whatever harsh words were said, whatever the wounds given and taken — Fanny had failed Camilla, and she had to know that. She was unsuited temperamentally to admitting even to herself that she had been wrong, but Camilla's death left her with a burden of guilt mixed with an irretrievable loss. It left her with a formidable psychic struggle for survival.

It would be foolish to imagine that Camilla's death was solely responsible for the ensuing misery in Fanny's life. That summer she married Phiquepal d'Arusmont, no doubt for the sake of their child's legitimacy. She had another daughter who died before she was four months old, and she assigned the birthdate of the second child to the first and maintained the lie all her life. It was one of the few things she set out to do that succeeded. But her marriage was disastrous, and within five years Fanny had lost or broken every friendship that had mattered to her when Camilla was alive.

Fanny survived Camilla by twenty years, but the record she left is very nearly opaque when one attempts to discover what she really felt. Everyone who wrote about her subsequently described a woman who was trying valiantly, but who seemed remote and unpredictable. She suffered a series of nervous breakdowns and apparently endured them for the most part alone. Her writing became too often puffy and vague, and her behavior alternately imperious and querulous.

The sisters had two decades together that were far richer than all but the rarest women's lives in the nineteenth century. They had seen so much of their world and had been feted by it with no common measure of praise. Still, the story of Fanny and Camilla Wright leaves me glad I have no natural sister. So interdependent were their lives that once one began to go, the other, it seemed, could only follow. No one can have paid a higher price than Fanny for the years she took Camilla for granted. I take no consolation in that fact. They were both beautiful young women who tried to live justly and with compassion. For the wretched tangle of loss and confusion and failure that their lives became I find no redeeming grace. I see only how fragile hope and goodness are and wonder how many can survive their loss, and to what end.

## NOTES

1. George Jacob Holyoake, *The History of Co-operation* (London: T. F. Unwin, 1908), I, 240–241.
2. Fanny Wright to Mary Wollstonecraft Shelley, 20 March 1828, *The Life and Letters of Mary Wollstonecraft Shelley*, ed. Mrs. Julian Marshall (1889; reprint ed., New York: Haskell House, 1970), II, 180.
3. Frances Wright, "Explanatory Notes on Nashoba," *New Harmony Gazette*, 30 Jan., 6 and 13 Feb. 1828.
4. Frances Wright, *England the Civilizer: Her History Developed in Its Principles* (London, 1848), pp. 13, 22.
5. Frances Wright, *Biography and Notes of Frances Wright D'Arusmont*, reprinted in Frances Wright, *Life, Letters and Lectures, 1834–1844* (New York: Arno Press, 1972), p. 9.
6. James Mylne to Mr. Watson, 15 July 1815, Theresa Wolfson Papers, Martin P. Catherwood Library, Cornell University.
7. Frederick Lamb to Lady Melbourne, n.d., quoted in William C. Lehmann, *John Millar of Glasgow, 1735–1801* (Cambridge: Cambridge University Press, 1960), p. 82.
8. Fanny Wright to Harriet Garnett, 7 July 1826, Garnett Letters, Houghton Library, Harvard University.
9. Camilla Wright to Julia Garnett, 10 Jan. 1826, Garnett Letters.
10. James Mylne to Julia Garnett, 12 Aug. 1827, Garnett Letters.
11. 15 Dec. 1827, Nashoba Book, Wolfson Papers.
12. Wright to Camilla Wright Whitby, 21 Feb. 1829, Wolfson Papers.
13. Camilla Wright Whitby to Julia Garnett Pertz, 19 Aug. 1829, Garnett Letters.
14. Camilla Wright Whitby to Harriet Garnett, copied in Garnett to Pertz, 16 Feb. 1830, Garnett Letters.
15. Fanny Wright to Robert Owen, 16 March 1831, Robert Owen Papers, Cooperative Union, Manchester, England.

# 5 No Connections Subsequent: Jane Austen's World of Sisterhood

Susan Sniader Lanser

> Children of the same family, the same blood, with the same first associations and habits, have some means of enjoyment in their power, which no subsequent connections can supply; and it must be by a long and unnatural estrangement, by a divorce which no subsequent connection can justify, if such precious remains of the earliest attachment are ever outlived. Too often, alas! it is so.
> — Jane Austen, *Mansfield Park* (Chapter 24)

This generalization by the narrator of *Mansfield Park* stands in startling contrast to the very *telos* of Austen's work. Indeed, the narrator's assertion seems more descriptive of Austen herself than of her characters, for while the dominant focus of the novels is the marriage quest, Austen's own story is one of sisterhood. Barring separations that were always involuntary and onerous, Jane Austen shared with her sister Cassandra bed, board, writings, and intimate thoughts from childhood until death. Austen's proclamation of sibling primacy in a novel whose closure is itself quasi-incestuous may help to illuminate the apparent dissonance between Austen's stories and her life.

The traditional approach to this dissonance — to infer a biography of disappointments in love — has been unwittingly encouraged by Cassandra herself. As Virginia Woolf writes:

> If Miss Cassandra Austen had had her way, we should have nothing of Jane Austen's except her novels. To elder sister alone did she write freely, to her alone she confided her hopes. . . . But when Miss Cassandra Austen grew old, and the growth of her sister's fame made her suspect that a time might come when strangers would pry and scholars speculate, she burnt, at great cost to herself, every letter that could gratify their curiosity, and spared only what she judged too trivial to be of interest.
>
> Hence our knowledge of Jane Austen is derived from a little gossip, a few letters, and her books.[1]

Inevitably these slender resources, if less paltry than Woolf implies, have been layered with fictions as biographers pry and speculate. Reading the life as if it were an Austen novel, some biographers have tried to ferret out relationships with men, to invent romantic sorrows or disasters that would synchronize Austen's own desires with those of her heroines. The evidence is clear, however, that what Cassandra sealed in silence were the secrets of two women whose intimacy and understanding equaled that of Austen's happiest marital pairs. Jane Austen's love for Cassandra, chosen from childhood, was not substitute but sustenance; it provided the spiritual and material support that made her writing possible.

53

The fictions stimulated by Cassandra's silence have impoverished not only biographical visions of Austen's life, but also critical readings of her works. By exploring Austen's novels in light of her own "primary relationship" of sisterhood, I am positing an alternative to the tradition that has examined these texts almost exclusively in terms of male-female relationships. Recognizing the importance of sisterhood to the novels themselves reinterprets the gap between text and life; at the same time it asks us to understand why Austen could have made the kind of generalization she offers in *Mansfield Park*, yet could not have inscribed the sister-plot that constitutes her own experience.

Such an inquiry must reevaluate as well the perception that women in Austen's novels lack a sense of (spiritual) sisterhood. Patricia Beer, for example, writes in *Reader, I Married Him*:

> What solidarity do Jane Austen's heroines display? The answer, unfortunately, is almost none. Some pairs of sisters give each other invaluable support — Jane and Elizabeth Bennet, Elinor and Marianne Dashwood — but Maria and Julia Bertram give way to the most unpleasant and spiteful rivalry. . . . Women friends and acquaintances consistently throw each other to the wolves.[2]

What Beer ignores here is the crucial correlation in Austen's world between sisterhood and integrity: Maria and Julia Bertram, after all, hardly count among "Jane Austen's heroines." A good woman, for Austen, is invariably a good sister, and a woman's defects are often signaled by her lack of sisterly concern. Thus all of Austen's heroines know — or learn — to be sisterly and are shocked by anything less; as Emma Watson says of her sister Penelope, "Could a sister do such a thing? — Rivalry, Treachery between sisters!"[3] Indeed, as Paula Bennett argues, in an Austen novel "the quality of an individual's relationships with his or her siblings is an indication of the quality of his or her character."[4] I would extend this to suggest that the quality of a woman's relationships to other women is similarly indicative: if she has indeed matured, Emma Woodhouse must become Jane Fairfax's friend.

In fact, the quest to forge, maintain, or recover a bond of sisterhood constitutes a quiet but persistent theme in virtually all of Austen's work, often paralleling and intertwining with the marital quest. In such early works as *Sense and Sensibility* and *Pride and Prejudice*, Austen creates double plots, generating marriages for the sisters that preserve the sisterhood; in later novels like *Mansfield Park* and *Persuasion*, the theme of sisterhood takes on symbolic roles. Shifting in nature and function with shifts in Austen's own life, sisterhood in Austen's novels constitutes the prototype for marriage itself; the ideal marriage, finally, may be modeled upon the ideal sisterhood.

In multiple ways, the imperatives of marriage and sisterhood were intertwined for Austen herself. Born not quite three years apart in 1773 and 1775, the only daughters in a clergyman's family of eight, Cassandra and Jane Austen were inseparable as children. When Cassandra was sent off to boarding school at the age of nine, Jane, though only six, went too, rather than be parted from the sister she adored. Their mother is said to have commented, "If Cassandra was going to have her head cut off, Jane would insist on sharing her fate." They also shared a bedroom and a bed during their childhood and apparently throughout their adult lives. While Jane wrote or played the piano, Cassandra painted and sketched; the Austen legacy includes Cassandra's portraits as well as Jane's texts. Family lore has it that Jane looked up to her elder and more reserved sibling, but that adoration was mutual and "affinity of spirit"[5] exceedingly strong. Even in the age of what Carroll Smith-Rosenberg has called "the female world of love and ritual,"[6] and even in a family where the bonds among siblings were strikingly close, the harmony between Jane and Cassandra was remarkable — and remarked upon.

It was in the shared bedroom that Jane's writings, from the early "juvenilia" to the last, unfinished *Sanditon*, received their first audience; Cassandra's encouragement was the heart of the familial support that nourished Jane's youthful efforts with the pen. The early stories, composed between Austen's twelfth and eighteenth years (and copied into three volumes that still exist), testify to Cassandra's special role in Jane's literary development: while most of the family members are graced by the dedication of one youthful text, Cassandra is honored with four (and provided the illustrations for at least one of these). Sister relationships are prominent in several of those early tales.

Of particular interest are two narratives dedicated to Cassandra and written about 1792, when Cassandra would have reached marriageable age. The first, a three-page extravaganza titled "The Beautifull Cassandra: A Novel in Twelve Chapters," is the only text Austen ever composed that makes use of her sister's first name.[7] A striking piece of adolescent wish-fulfillment, it takes its heroine on an unconventional picaresque journey which, after seven hours, happily leads her home again. In the interval, she has fallen in love, but with a pretty hat rather than the handsome Viscount who approaches her. Her activities are capricious and unfeminine: striking the pastry cook, gorging on ices, hiring a coach for an aimless and scandalously solitary ride. The psychological counterpoint to this tale is the more conventional "Catherine, or the Bower," in which two daughters of a clergyman are separated by their parents' death and their consequent impoverishment. The elder is forced to be "splendidly, yet unhappily married" to a man twice her age whom she despises and who takes her off to India;[8] the younger is forced to serve a rich relative and pines for the sister she has lost. Between them, then, "The Beautifull Cassandra" [sic] and "Catherine" imagine the best and worst fates for Cassandra and Jane.

The biographical reality was, of course, somewhere in between. We will never know how Jane responded when, in 1795, Cassandra became engaged. Austen biographer Jane Aiken Hodge speculates that "for the first time she would have found herself taking second place in the beloved sister's affections. It must have been very lonely, all of a sudden, in the shared bedroom at Steventon."⁹ Jane may never have taken second place in Cassandra's affections; one must remember that in households of the Austens' modest means, "sisters were expected to marry and relieve their families of responsibility for their maintenance."¹⁰ But surely Jane dreaded the marriage that should eventually take Cassandra away forever. Life without sisterhood was put to the test when, soon after her engagement, Cassandra paid a long visit to her fiancé Tom Fowle's family in Berkshire, while Fowle himself was off seeking his fortune in the West Indies. Not coincidentally, Jane's letters of these months brag to Cassandra about a flirtation with another Tom, Tom Lefroy.

Cassandra destroyed many of the letters that might describe the sisters' life during the months of her engagement and the period just after February 1797 when news came that Tom Fowle had died of malaria. But it is during these years that Jane drafted the novels that would become her first two published books: "Elinor and Marianne," revised as *Sense and Sensibility*, and "First Impressions," which became *Pride and Prejudice*. These novels, Hodge speculates, were begun "in the loneliness of Cassandra's engagement" and became "a distraction . . . in her bereavement" (p. 51). Both *Sense and Sensibility* and *Pride and Prejudice* structure their marriage quests in doubled—and sistered—form; both, indeed, seem organized by an imperative to reconcile marriage and sisterhood. Each novel creates a pair of devoted sisters who are superior to the other members of their family and complementary in temperament. The love quests of the sisters intertwine, and the resolutions to both stories ensure the happiness not only of marriage but of sisterhood.

In *Sense and Sensibility* the elder sister, Elinor, plays a central role in the development of the younger, Marianne. Marianne's love and admiration for Elinor need no improvement, however; when it appears, early in the book, that Elinor will soon marry, Marianne frets,

> "Oh! Mama, how shall we do without her?"
> "My love, it will be scarcely a separation. We shall live within a few miles of each other and shall meet every day of our lives." (Ch. 3)

When she learns that there is as yet no engagement, Marianne is relieved that "*I* shall not lose you so soon" (Ch. 4). Even at her most foolish, Marianne's "affectionate heart" cannot "bear to see a sister slighted in the smallest point" (Ch. 34). Marianne's growth can ultimately be measured by her regret that she has not followed her sister's counsel, by her recognition that Elinor "'above all, above my mother, (has) been wronged by me. . . . Your example was before me; but to what avail'" (Ch. 46). As she grows in wisdom, then, Marianne also grows in similarity to Elinor, a growth stimulated by her chagrin at "the comparison . . . between Elinor's conduct and her own" (Ch. 38).

In resolving the double plot of *Sense and Sensibility*, Austen rewards both sisters not only with worthy mates, but with lifelong sisterhood. It is significant, however, that in this first-published novel, she betrays visible discomfort in doing so. The very last sentence of the book announces that

> among the merits and the happiness of Elinor and Marianne, let it *not* be ranked as the *least* considerable, that *though* sisters, and living almost within sight of each other, they could live *without* disagreement between themselves, or producing coolness between their husbands. (Ch. 50, emphases mine)

Since Elinor and Marianne have never really quarreled, and indeed Marianne has seen her sister as her "'only comfort,'" Austen's language here, however ironic, bows to the convention of sister as rival in a way that the text itself does not. The passage suggests Austen's ambivalence at giving sisterhood the last and unconventional word in *Sense and Sensibility*.

Austen goes on, nonetheless, to reinscribe the sister-plot in *Pride and Prejudice*, forging a still deeper relationship between the imperatives of marriage and sisterhood and reversing the plot of rescue. While in the first novel it is the elder sister who saves the younger, in *Pride and Prejudice* the act of redemption, if not of education, belongs to the younger sister: Elizabeth saves the older and (she believes) nobler Jane from despair by intervening, through Darcy, in Jane's love affair with Bingley.[11] In relation to the biography, it would be interesting to know whether Jane Bennet was created before or after Tom Fowle's death, which Cassandra reportedly accepted with a silent fortitude similar to Jane's forbearance of Bingley's perplexing abandonment.

In *Pride and Prejudice* the sister-bond, which is even closer than that in *Sense and Sensibility*, moves into the foreground of the plot by generating both its complications and its resolution. Preferring the sister to the man, Elizabeth at first rejects Darcy because she has learned that he "congratulated himself" for "saving" his friend Bingley "from the inconvenience of a most imprudent marriage" to Jane; as Elizabeth asks him, "'Do you think that any consideration would tempt me to accept the man who has been the means of ruining, perhaps for ever, the happiness of a most beloved sister?'" (Chs. 33, 34). Only when Darcy's intervention has in fact ensured Bingley's proposal and Jane's happiness (as well as sister Lydia's virtue and the family's honor) does Elizabeth accept Darcy and secure her own future. Indeed, Jane also requires her sister's happiness: she says to Elizabeth when Darcy has proposed, "'Now I am quite happy, for you will be as happy as myself'" (Ch. 59). Austen also strengthens the interrelationship of sister-plot and marriage-plot by making Darcy and Bingley close friends whose complementarity is not unlike that of Jane and Elizabeth, and who would naturally want to settle in neighboring shires. The result is that Jane and Elizabeth, "in addition to every other source of happiness, were within thirty miles of each other" (Ch. 61). Such an understatement provides, if more subtly than the negative language of *Sense and Sensibility*, another sign of the narrator's discomfort at making sisterhood figure centrally in the story's end.

It is significant that the only two of Austen's novels that create parallel plots reconciling marriage and sisterhood were conceived during the two-year period when Cassandra was engaged. In fact, the threat of separation through marriage continued to be at least theoretically possible for another decade. Temporary separations, often for months at a time, were continuous during these years, usually because Cassandra was sent to help various sisters-in-law when a new baby arrived. It is clear from the surviving correspondence that these separations were ill-borne at least by Jane, that letters were exchanged several times a week — frequently enough to attract notice — and that their contents were kept in strict confidence on both sides. Jane's letters to Cassandra are sprinkled with chidings for not hearing from her even more frequently and with longings for Cassandra's return. The letters give little support to speculations that Jane had serious suitors during this time (though the letters are, of course, mightily pruned); there are some comments indicating boredom with (and even contempt for) the men Jane Austen encountered at balls and social gatherings. Jane Hodge suspects that the repeated separations imposed by the family on Cassandra and Jane were consciously designed to keep them apart long enough for each to find a mate. They "must have made a fairly formidable combination," Hodge speculates:

> If Jane dismissed the young men she met at balls as not 'good for much,' what did they think of Jane? And if there was a dangerous hint of laughter about her when she went to balls alone, what in the world can she and Cassandra have been like together? Even the best of good manners cannot quite hide the delicious complicity of a shared joke. (p. 75)

Finding husbands for Jane and Cassandra may also have motivated the Austen family's sudden decision in 1800 to leave Steventon Rectory, their Hampshire home for over thirty years, to settle in the popular resort town of Bath. Jane was deeply attached to Steventon, detested Bath, and allegedly fainted at the news. But she was already twenty-four and Cassandra twenty-seven; there was not much time left. Indeed, family lore has it that two possibilities did surface briefly in the next two years. In 1801 during a three-week vacation Austen allegedly met a young man who showed great interest in her, but within a matter of months he apparently died. The following year brought the one proposal of marriage Austen is known to have received, though the man was not a connection made in Bath but an old friend whose sisters Jane and Cassandra were visiting in Hampshire. The consensus is that one evening during the visit the brother, Harris Bigg Wither, asked Jane to marry him and received her consent. But the next morning, Jane and Cassandra turned up distraught and tearful at the nearby house of their brother James, insisting with uncharacteristic disregard for the inconvenience to his clerical responsibilities that he accompany them back to Bath. Jane had retracted the engagement and was so wretched that she had to return home at once.

Circumstantially speaking it would have been a good match. Harris Bigg

Wither, though slightly younger than Jane, was intelligent, congenial, and rich; his two sisters were close friends of Cassandra and Jane; the marriage would have allowed Jane to return to her beloved Hampshire; and after her parents' death, to quote biographer Elizabeth Jenkins, she would have been able "to offer the security of a home to the person [Cassandra] she loved best on earth."[12] But it would not have been a marriage of love, and the task of supervising an affluent household would surely have put an end to writing for the woman who found composition "impossible with a head full of joints of mutton and doses of rhubarb."

This moment was thus a personal and professional turning point. Whatever opportunities for marriage had or had not existed earlier, this time Jane Austen was *choosing* spinsterhood, which also meant choosing poverty, insecurity, social inferiority, and dependence on familial generosity for her support. On the other side, it meant choosing sisterhood and choosing literature. Jane Hodge speculates:

> When [Austen] refused Harris Bigg Wither after what must have been a sleepless night, she knew exactly what she was doing. She was condemning herself to a lifetime as a second class citizen, an object of contemptuous humor, as an old maid. She was also condemning herself to write *Emma, Mansfield Park*, and *Persuasion*, and we must be grateful to her, and to Cassandra, who undoubtedly made it possible. If there had been no Cassandra, I imagine there would have been no sleepless night, and a large family of extremely intelligent little Bigg Withers. (p. 83)

Whatever was said and felt during that imagined sleepless night, from that time, Mrs. Austen declared, "Jane and Cassandra were wedded to each other." To this Jane Hodge adds, "It was a happy marriage and a productive one," and quotes Jane's reference to *Pride and Prejudice* as "my own darling child."[13]

The combined state of singlehood and sisterhood clearly provided the material situation that made Jane Austen's literary career possible. While as a married woman Jane would have been bound to keep house, it was Cassandra who managed their household so that Jane could write. Spinsterhood also gave Austen's writing an economic imperative that marriage would have erased, and her reticence to announce herself an author might have kept her texts unpublished had financial need not intervened. While her works were never best-sellers, her letters and ledgers show that her earnings were significant both psychologically and materially. It is probably no coincidence, then, that within a year after this turning point of the refused engagement the manuscript of *Northanger Abbey* was sold to a publisher. Meanwhile, Austen continued to write, composing or recopying two of her harshest works, *The Watsons* and *Lady Susan*, both of which stress the bitter economic straits of women's lives.

*The Watsons*, the only text whose composition can be attributed definitively to the relatively silent period in Austen's life that began the new century, inaugurates a change in Austen's mode of inscribing sisterhood. As in *Sense and Sensibility* and *Pride and Prejudice*, Austen creates a family of daughters (and one son who considers his sisters "a weight upon your family") in which two sisters, Elizabeth and Emma, form the superior pair. Reunited after a separation of many years, the sisters are quite content with their own "tranquil and affectionate intercourse," as their "mutual regard was increasing with the intimate knowledge of each other which such intercourse produced" (p. 348). But in *The Watsons* Austen ruptures the plot of the double marriage by creating an elder sister (another Elizabeth) who, at twenty-eight (near Austen's age at the time) has (perhaps like Cassandra) already loved and lost. Yet Elizabeth insists:

> "we must marry. — I could do very well single for my own part — A little Company, & a pleasant Ball now & then, would be enough for me, if one could be young for ever, but my Father cannot provide for us, & it is very bad to grow old & be poor & laughed at. — I have lost Purvis, it is true but very few people marry their first Loves. I should not refuse a man because he was not Purvis." (p. 317)

The sisters wonder whether it is better to become a teacher — "'& I can think,'" says Emma, "'of nothing worse'" — or to marry a man one does not love. In a tone distant indeed from the romantic optimism of the earlier sister-novels, *The Watsons* presents sisterhood as emotional sufficiency but marriage as economic imperative. Austen never finished this novel, perhaps because of its bleak and untempered social criticism, but family lore suggests she had planned an ending not unlike the one a marriage to Harris Bigg Wither would have secured for her and Cassandra: Elizabeth remains single, but Emma, nine years her junior, marries a nobleman and, presumably, provides a home for Elizabeth.

The Austen sisters' own financial plight worsened sharply after their father's death in 1805, an event that also left their mother's care entirely in their hands. It is clear that neither sister was close to Mrs. Austen and that they found her presence somewhat burdensome, but there was no morally or economically feasible way to live apart from her. Jane Hodge comments:

> There was no possible escape, even if they had been so heartless as to consider it. . . . Aristocrats, like the ladies of Llangollen, might possibly set up housekeeping together, . . . but for young women of the middle class it was, simply, impossible. . . . The Austen brothers might subsidize the respectable household of a mother and sisters, but they would never have supported a breakaway. (p. 111).

Ironically, it was the desire to live *à deux* that led Cassandra and Jane to add a fourth member to their *ménage à trois* by inviting their unmarried friend Martha Lloyd, whose mother had just died, to live with them. Martha and Jane were especially close; Jenkins attributes it to the "reasonable nature of

Jane's and Cassandra's attachment . . . that, singularly profound as it was, they welcomed" Martha's joining them.[14] But Martha's presence also allowed them to go off visiting together instead of leaving Jane behind with Mrs. Austen. And when Cassandra went alone, Jane would have Martha for company. Letters confirm that the threesome was a cozy one, and even with Martha in the house there was always the privacy of Jane and Cassandra's shared room.

Such was the household constellation in 1808 when the Austens moved to Chawton Cottage in Hampshire, where they would remain. Here Jane Austen's literary career entered full bloom. While Cassandra managed the household, Jane revised the early novels and wrote all the later works, for which Cassandra was first reader and critic. Absences continued to be borne badly, at least by Jane; when Cassandra was away in 1817 Jane was still writing that she would "grudge every half day wasted on the road" till Cassandra's return.[15]

While the relationship between the sisters, so far as we can construct it, remained constant during these productive years, the story of the sister-pair dissolves from the novels once Austen's own "marriage" to Cassandra, with its literary progeny, is assured. But Austen continues to create structures that intertwine marriage quests with the search for sisterhood as sisterly bonds are forged, through marriage itself, between sisters-in-law. Catherine Moreland is as much attracted to Eleanor Tilney as to Eleanor's brother Henry; Elizabeth Bennet is just the sister Darcy wants for Georgiana. Austen often prefigures the unsuitability of a marriage by showing the unsuitability of a sisterhood. In *Northanger Abbey*, Isabella Thorpe becomes engaged to Catherine Moreland's brother James and hopes that a double union will be achieved through Catherine's marriage to her (boorish) brother John. Isabella's unsuitability as a sister is indeed suggested by her outspoken preference of Catherine to her own sisters: "'You will be so infinitely dearer to me, my Catherine, than either Anne or Maria: I feel that I shall be so much more attached to my dear Morland's family than to my own'" (Ch. 15). Both marriages are averted in favor of the Tilney match; Catherine's movement away from the Thorpes and toward the Tilneys is the mark of her growing maturity. In *Mansfield Park*, Fanny Price is similarly unwilling to form a sisterly bond with Mary Crawford (also Fanny's rival for the love of Edmund), whose unprincipled brother Henry is seeking Fanny's hand. Like Isabella, Mary presses the bond, insisting that "'I know we shall [be sisters]. I feel that we were born to be connected; and . . . you feel it too'" (Ch. 36). The sisterly bonds Austen's heroines do forge with their sisters-in-law serve to strengthen the superior familial networks that marriages in Austen's novels usually constitute and provide heroines with sisterly ties when they must leave home.

This symbolic role of the sister, whose presence or absence reflects the fate of a family and the vitality of the "estate," which, in turn, represents English society as a whole, constitutes the central function of sisterhood in two of

Austen's last three novels, *Mansfield Park* and *Persuasion*. As Alistair Duckworth has shown, most of Austen's novels, and particularly these two, can be said to confront the questions: "Who shall inherit England? How shall we improve the estate?"[16] Typically, Austen's answer involves a strengthening of England's future through a rising and hard-working middle class. In *Mansfield Park* and *Persuasion* sisterhood remains an important element of the heroine's happiness but also figures in the larger social movement that the novels portray.

*Mansfield Park* may appear to be much more concerned with brotherhood than with sisterhood, for its heroine, Fanny Price, adores her brother William and marries his closest counterpart, the cousin in whose home she has been raised. There are in fact incestuous implications to both relationships; when William visits Mansfield, for example, he longs to dance with Fanny once more, and argues that "nobody would know who I was here" (Ch. 25). For most of the novel Fanny appears to be sisterless: Certainly her cousins Maria and Julia Bertram are unwilling to befriend her, and when she returns to her childhood home we learn that her favorite sister, Mary, has died some years before. But the resolution of *Mansfield Park*, which secures both Fanny's happiness and the "improvement of the estate," makes significant use of the sisterbond.

It is when Fanny has reached a nadir of isolation and despair that Austen provides her with the solace of sisterhood. Having finally achieved a place of value at Mansfield, she now seems to have lost everything: Mansfield, Edmund, the Crawfords, Sir Thomas, the countryside, sympathy, quiet, and gentility. Exiled to the squalor of her natal home in Portsmouth, deprived even of William, who is at sea, Fanny discovers a peer in her younger sister, Susan. Susan, who is paid the ultimate compliment of being "like William," is superior to the rest of the Prices in almost every way, and thus "very little better fitted for home than her elder sister" (Ch. 43). (Interestingly, Susan pays Fanny, as Jane paid Cassandra and Cassandra must surely have paid Jane, "the compliment of preferring her style to that of any printed author" [Ch. 43]). At Portsmouth Susan is Fanny's "only companion and listener," "always ready to hear and to sympathize" (Ch. 44). Fanny recognizes Susan as her more energetic and assertive double: "Susan was only acting on the same truths . . . which her own judgement acknowledged, but which her more supine and yielding temper would have shrunk from asserting" (Ch. 40). The "intimacy thus begun between them" provides a bulwark against the Price household; "by sitting together upstairs" in their shared chamber, often reading the books that Fanny has procured for them, Fanny and Susan "avoided a great deal of the disturbance of the house" (Ch. 40).

Unwittingly, Fanny is readying Susan to take her place at Mansfield Park as a stronger version of herself. The resolution of the novel, in which the unworthy members of the family are exiled and the worthy "poor relations" brought in to shore up the ailing estate, is consolidated most of all by Fanny's marriage to her cousin Edmund. Since Fanny and Edmund are to be installed at Mansfield's parsonage, it would not be essential for Austen to replace Fanny at Mansfield Park. Yet Fanny is asked to bring Susan back to Mansfield "to supply her place"; Susan is in fact "established at Mansfield with every appearance of equal permanency" and ultimately becomes "perhaps the most beloved of the two" (Ch. 48). The two Price sisters thus replace the errant Maria and Julia Bertram as the true heirs to the estate. It is even possible that the inclusion of Susan as Fanny's double is intended to generate a repetition of the central plot: perhaps the comment about Susan's "permanency" at Mansfield Park implies that she will secure the future by marrying the other Bertram son, Tom, the reformed and lawful heir.

If *Mansfield Park* uses sisterhood to consolidate the estate, *Persuasion* uses the absence of sisterhood to figure its abandonment. Anne Elliott is the most alienated and isolated of Austen's heroines; her loneliness grows not only from the loss of a love that the novel will restore to her, but from the loss of sisterhood as well. Like the prototypical Romantic hero, Anne is set apart and devalued by her family; only her mother, many years deceased, would have been her spiritual peer. Fitted, as it were, with a sister on either side, Anne remains the neglected middle. With her older sister, Elizabeth, as with her father, she "was nobody: her word had no weight, her convenience was always to give way" (Ch. 1). Her younger sister, Mary, an incompetent housekeeper and mother given to depression and hypochondria, summons and uses shamelessly the maiden aunt who is assumed to have no life of her own. Anne's isolation leads her to envy the Musgrove sisters, although she knows they are not her equals; while she "would not have given up her own more elegant and cultivated mind for all their enjoyments," she longs for "that seemingly perfect good understanding and agreement together, that good-humored mutual affection, of which she had known so little herself with either of her sisters" (Ch. 5). When her former love, Captain Wentworth, returns after an eight-year absence, he will rescue her as much from the lack of sisterhood as from the state of spinsterhood. In a symbolic episode, Wentworth is the only person who can remove literally from Anne's back her sister's two-year-old son, symbolically rescuing her from her isolation within the family, from her sister's exploitation, and from the fate of the maiden aunt. When Anne and Wentworth marry, Anne's only sorrow is that she has "no relations to bestow on him which a man of sense could value . . . no family to receive and estimate him properly" (Ch. 24). She will perhaps find a new sense of sisterhood with Mrs. Croft, Wentworth's sister, who has, significantly, moved into the Elliot family home of Kellynch Hall after Anne's father ran up debts and was forced to lease it. Anne alone is worthy of the estate; no sister can accompany her return to Kellynch.

In this last novel, then, Austen finds an objective correlative for Anne Elliot's Romantic alienation not only in the absence of a spouse, but in the absence of a sister, the two losses constituting parallel abandonments that are partly restored by Anne's marriage to Wentworth. At the same time, the absence of a worthy sister marks a loss of faith in the possibility of broad unions across social class. As Fanny's bringing a sister marked the solidification of the estate, so Anne's need to leave her family behind marks Austen's virtual abandonment of the nobility in favor of the new class of naval officers. Unlike the earlier novels, *Persuasion* inscribes the theme of sisterhood by showing the loneliness its absence generates.

In this last finished novel, then, Austen creates her only heroine whose biological sisters have abandoned all sense of sisterhood. Perhaps it is not irrelevant that by this time Austen herself is facing the possibility of eternal separation from her own sister; written during the illness from which she would die less than a year later, *Persuasion* may reflect its author's own sense of isolation and sisterly loss. Eight months after finishing *Persuasion*, in April 1817, Austen took permanently to her bed (suffering from what has been posthumously described as Addison's disease) and made a will leaving Cassandra all her earthly goods.

As the illness wore on and death grew imminent, the snug cottage at Chawton may have seemed too small for nursing an invalid, and Cassandra and Jane wished to spare their 77-year-old mother the anguish of watching her daughter die. They also wanted to avail themselves of the medical care offered only in larger towns, and they may have as well wanted to be alone. For on 24 May 1817, leaving Martha to look after Mrs. Austen, Jane and Cassandra traveled by carriage to Winchester, and there remained together, Cassandra nursing Jane through her remaining months. On July 17 Cassandra went into town on an errand for Jane and returned to find her sister faint and suffering. Cassandra asked if she wanted anything; Jane said she wanted nothing but death. By evening she was unconscious. Cassandra sat for six hours with a pillow on her lap to support Jane's head. Her sister-in-law Mary came and relieved her for two hours. Then, at 3:30 a.m., Cassandra came back, and an hour later, on Friday, July 18, Jane Austen died in her sister's arms.

It is ironic that Cassandra, the ruthless preserver of her sister's privacy, left a record of her love for Jane that is more revealing than the record she left us of Jane's love for her. She writes to their favorite niece, Fanny, in a rare moment of candor just after Jane's death:

> I *have* lost a treasure, such a Sister, such a friend, as never can have been surpassed, — she was the sun of my life, the gilder of every pleasure, the soother of every sorrow, I had not a thought concealed from her, & it is as if I had lost a part of myself. I loved her only too well, not better than she deserved, but I am conscious that my affection for her made me sometimes unjust to and negligent of others, & I can acknowledge, more than as a general principle, the justice of the hand which has struck this blow.[17]

She reported herself "perfectly conscious of the extent of my irreparable loss," but prayed "that I may never cease to reflect on her as inhabiting heaven, and never cease my humble endeavors (when it shall please God) to join her there." It did not "please God" for another twenty-eight years. Through all that time Cassandra seems never to have stopped missing Jane; her niece Caroline attests that "the most perfect affection and confidence ever subsisted between them, and great and lasting was the sorrow of the survivor when the final separation was made."[18] Elizabeth Jenkins reports that relatives, visiting Cassandra when she was very old, "were struck, when [she] spoke of her sister, by 'the accent of *living* love' in her voice."[19]

Love for Cassandra also lives in Jane Austen's voice, both above and beneath the surfaces of Austen's marriage plots. That the novels focus overtly on marriage is not surprising. In Austen's day, a woman's economic and social well-being virtually demanded that she marry. The conventions of social life, as Austen herself recognized, made the single woman, especially if she were poor, a target of ridicule, hardly a fit subject for serious literature. If anything, the conventions of fiction were even more conservative: novels of the eighteenth century, with few exceptions,[20] defined the heroine (and hero*ine* she was) in terms of romantic intrigue; other women figured primarily as chaperones, rivals, and confidantes whose presence supported the heterosexual plot. Louisa Alcott's classic sister-story, *Little Women* (which also bows to the convention of marriage) was still half a century away. Had Austen even imagined the possibility of writing stories about contented single women with close female relationships, she would have earned hardly a shilling for her effort. Aesthetically, economically, socially, and perhaps psychologically, Austen's own experience could not yet be inscribed in fictional terms.

It is therefore significant that just as Austen manages to stretch if not to break conventions of narrative method, of ideology and character, so too does she stretch her plots to create unconventionally strong sisterhoods, both biological and spiritual. Since the relationship between the Austen sisters seems to have been ideal, it should not be surprising that Austen's novels ultimately blur the qualitative distinctions between the love of married partners and the love of sisters. Both clearly require the same qualities of warmth, complementarity, honesty, loyalty, and intelligence.

Some of the novels seem indeed to constitute marriages for which sisterhood provides the mold. In *Sense and Sensibility*, for example, Marianne's education effects a change in her desire: while she had been in love with Willoughby, the scoundrel who was much like her romantic "former" self in temperament, she ultimately finds happiness with the quiet, steadfast if unexciting Colonel Brandon, a man much like Elinor. The marriages of Jane and Elizabeth Bennet also show their attraction to the sister's temperament: Bingley is described as lively, open, and at ease — much like Elizabeth — while Darcy is proud, reticent, and easy to misjudge — like Jane. The marriages thus replicate both the sisterly relationship and the friendship between the men, suggesting that, ideally, relationships of friends, siblings, and spouses are not all that dissimilar. Similarly, Austen forms marriages on the basis of brother-sister bonds: Not long before Edmund proposes to Fanny, he calls her "'My Fanny, my only sister; my only comfort now!'" (Ch. 46); Emma Woodhouse marries the man whose brother has already married her own sister Isabella. And Austen continually refuses to let her heroic characters marry purely on the basis of romantic attraction, stressing instead companionship and quality of character.

It is highly likely, then, that Jane Austen's own lifelong relationship with Cassandra did constitute the mold of the "perfect" marriage with which Austen's heroines are ultimately rewarded. That the reward takes the form of marriage rather than sisterhood cannot be surprising: Jane Austen was nothing if not a realist.[21] But if sisterhood does constitute the model of marital happiness, then Jane Austen's relationship with Cassandra moves from the background to the center of every novel she ever wrote. If this is the case, there is far less disparity between Jane Austen's life and her works than the fictional surfaces would suggest, and the incestuous structure of a novel like *Mansfield Park* lays bare the author's desire to figure her own experience as best she might. A reading of texts against biography yields one more way in which Austen's fictional surfaces are deceptive, in which, as Virginia Woolf said, Austen's writing "stimulates us to supply what is not there."[22] In censoring her sister's letters, then, Cassandra did with Jane's life what Jane did with her fictions: left us a legacy of covers and silences. This is surely fitting for two sisters who understood one another so well.

## NOTES

1. Virginia Woolf, "Jane Austen," in *The Common Reader*, First Series (New York: Harcourt Brace World, 1925), p. 137.
2. Patricia Beer, *Reader, I Married Him* (New York: Barnes and Noble, 1974), p. 76.
3. Jane Austen, "The Watsons," in *The Works of Jane Austen*, ed. R. W. Chapman (London: Oxford University Press, 1954), Vol. VI, p. 316. References to the juvenilia and to unfinished works will be taken from this edition. For the six completed novels, which exist in countless editions, I have cited only the chapter.
4. Paula Bennett, abstract for "Family Relationships in the Novels of Jane Austen," Dissertation, University of Washington, 1980, in *Dissertation Abstracts* 41 (11), 4717A.
5. The phrase is David Cecil's (*A Portrait of Jane Austen* [New York: Hill and Wang, 1978], p. 45).
6. Carroll Smith-Rosenberg, "The Female World of Love and Ritual: Relationships between Women in Nineteenth Century America," *Signs* 1, 1 (1975): 1–29. Although Smith-Rosenberg writes here about American women, her findings seem descriptive of British women in Austen's day.
7. Accidentally or purposefully, Austen gave her characters the names of family members and close friends and of Austen herself. The exception, Cassandra, is

the name of both Austen's sister and her mother. Sister Cassandra's middle name, Elizabeth, was used frequently by Austen; Jane and Elizabeth are of course the names of the extremely loyal sister-heroines of *Pride and Prejudice*.

8. Austen, *The Works of Jane Austen*, VI, p. 194.
9. Jane Aiken Hodge, *Only A Novel: The Double Life of Jane Austen* (New York: Coward McCann Geoghegan, 1972), p. 43. Further references to this work will appear in parentheses in the body of the text.
10. Kathleen Freeman, *T'other Miss Austen* (London: Macdonald, 1956), p. 42.
11. Notably, Austen here inverts the names and ages of the sisters from their (possible) autobiographical roots: the elder is Jane and the younger (Cassandra?) Elizabeth.
12. Elizabeth Jenkins, *Jane Austen* (New York: Pellegrini and Cudahy, 1949), p. 147.
13. Hodge, *Only a Novel*, p. 82. The comment about her "own darling child" comes from a letter to Cassandra of 29 January 1813 (in *Jane Austen's Letters*, ed. R. W. Chapman, 2nd ed. [London: Oxford University Press, 1952], p. 297).
14. Jenkins, *Jane Austen*, p. 165. The letters confirm Jane and Cassandra's willingness to incorporate Martha into their intimate circle. Jane wrote to Cassandra on November 20, 1800: "Martha desires her best love, and will be happy to welcome any letter from you to this house, whether it be addressed to herself or to me— and in fact, the difference of direction will not be material." This suggests that Jane and Cassandra considered Martha an intimate privileged like no other to share some part of their correspondence. In 1799 Jane had written to Cassandra that she'd spent a night visiting Martha, and that "I love Martha more than ever."
15. Letter of 8 September 1816, in *Letters*, p. 463.
16. Alistair Duckworth, *The Improvement of the Estate: A Study of Jane Austen's Novels* (Baltimore: Johns Hopkins University Press, 1977).
17. Letter of Cassandra Austen to Fanny Knight, in *Letters*, pp. 513–514.
18. Caroline Austen, *My Aunt Jane Austen. A Memoir* (London: Spottswoode, Ballantyne & Co., 1952), p. 11.
19. Jenkins, *Jane Austen*, p. 399.
20. Mary Wollstonecraft was one of the few women before Austen who explicitly set out to create autonomous female characters.
21. One could argue, of course, that it is hardly realistic to posit idealized marital relationships that are, in fact, based on sisterhood. Austen does not seem to have thought well of most of the marriages she observed.
22. Woolf, "Jane Austen," p. 142.

# 6 Florence Nightingale and the Bonds of Sisterhood

Sylvia Strauss

Florence Nightingale became a legend in her own time. After her triumphal return from the Crimea in 1856, she was the Lady with the Lamp, a "ministering angel." She was the ideal of nineteenth-century womanhood who comforted and nurtured the sick, and who sacrificed her own well-being for others. Songs such as *The Shadow on the Pillow* and *The Soldier's Cheer* were dedicated to her, as well as ballads and poems.

Legions of mothers named their daughters Florence in hopes that they would live up to the standards she set. In the nineteenth-century view, she accomplished extraordinary achievements without compromising her womanhood or her respectability, and in 1907, three years before her death, she received the Order of Merit from Edward VII, the first woman to be so honored.

The more cynical age of the twentieth century, attuned to the subterranean depths of the unconscious, has seen Nightingale in a different mold. Lytton Strachey was the first of the revisionists.[1] To Strachey, she was a veritable "demon" in pursuit of her goals, a single-minded obsessive who spared no one to accomplish her reforms. A more recent biography, *Florence Nightingale: Reputation and Power* by F. B. Smith (1982), accuses Nightingale of having an ego, of being tough, and seeking power through manipulative means. Her critics agree that the power she sought was used for highly laudatory purposes; that she must be credited with bringing about — or at least hastening — much needed improvements in the British army medical department and in hospital nursing. They agree that if she demanded much of others, least of all she spared herself as she poured out the statistics and reports that brought about far-reaching reforms. Neither do her contemporary critics question that she did more for women in opening up a remunerative and respectable profession — that of nursing — than the vaunted feminists of the nineteenth century who organized and made public speeches for the vote. She herself did not become active in the women's movement, although she had an abiding interest in the Woman Question. Her attitude to feminism can best be characterized as ambivalent. Florence Nightingale, it becomes increasingly evident, was a bundle of contradictions. An understanding of her can do much to clarify the confusions many women feel today as they seek to resolve the dilemmas that feminism poses for them.

The key to Florence Nightingale's outlook is her relationship to her sister Parthenope. It was a relationship characterized by hostility and resentment during their formative years and into adulthood, but became one that mellowed. They became closer in later life as each achieved her own goals and no longer tried to battle the other into submission.

Florence and Parthenope Nightingale grew up in the early nineteenth century, when marriage was the only proper and acceptable goal for women. At the same time, middle- and upper-class women were growing restive under such constraints and increasingly aware of the disabilities marriage imposed upon them. Once married, upper middle-class and aristocratic women were expected to devote themselves to their husbands and serve their husbands' ambitions. They were to command their servants and oversee the moral training of their children. They were to grace the husband's table and dress in order to please. They were encouraged to do needlework; to dabble in drawing, music, and painting; to read and write letters and to visit, thereby maintaining their social connections.

To put the matter succinctly, Parthenope Nightingale accepted the dictates of conventional society on women; Florence did not. Both were imbued with deep conflicts because of their differing inclinations. Florence Nightingale and her sister Parthenope were born into an upper-class aristocratic family. They were the daughters of William Edward Nightingale (W. E. N.) and Fanny Smith Nightingale. Both girls were born on the Continent during a leisurely honeymoon trip the newly married Nightingales were taking; both were named after the cities in which they were born. Parthenope is the Greek name for Naples, where she first saw the light of day in 1819; Florence was born in that Renaissance city in 1820. After three years abroad, the Nightingales returned to England to lead a life of leisure and indolence characteristic of the upper classes. The Nightingale family spent summers at their estate in Lea Hurst in Derbyshire; winters at Embly Park in Hampshire. The social season in spring and fall found them in London.

There is evidence that at an early age Florence Nightingale found her life empty and stultifying. She recorded that she had an early obsession that she was not like other children and felt isolated and alone.[2] She thought herself to be a monster as she engaged in a struggle to transcend the privileged trivial life that few in her immediate circle — least of all Parthenope — ever questioned. Florence's feeling of isolation was reinforced by the antagonisms her difference created with her mother and sister.

Current psychology would demand some examination of how the two little girls related to each other, to their parents, and to their circumstances in what are regarded as the formative years of life. According to psychological theory, Parthenope, the elder girl, should have set the pace for the younger, acquiring a greater confidence and a stronger identity. Perhaps a year's seniority is not enough time to develop that sense of specialness characteristic of an older child who has the parents' concentrated attention. But it was Florence who developed a sense of uniqueness, who saw herself as having a special calling; and it was Parthenope who felt resentment, envy, and jealousy — feelings exacerbated because they were repressed.

W. E. N., the girls' father, played a pivotal role in this regard. He was a country gentleman, who dabbled in Liberal politics. At one point he ran for Parliament but was defeated; from then on he spent his life tending his estates. He engaged in the hunting that was part of the aristocratic lifestyle, but was more cultivated than most members of his class and enjoyed reading in his large library. W. E. N. found little intellectual companionship in his wife, who was typical of her class, and thus responded to the curiosity of both his daughters, especially to Florence, who attached herself to him with deep passion and appeared to him the more comely as well as the brighter of the two girls. The partiality of W. E. N. for Florence caused Parthe, as she was nicknamed, to internalize her father's feelings and become an avid admirer and follower of her sister. However, she also felt resentment, which she was not able to articulate. When W. E. N. decided that his daughters' education could not be left in the hands of governesses, themselves for the most part ignorant, and that he himself would undertake the task of providing them with a classical education, the girls were further estranged. Parthe was quite bored trying to absorb history and conjugate Latin verbs; increasingly she preferred the passive, routinized, domestic world of her mother.

Florence flourished under her father's tutelage. As a result, she never considered herself the intellectual inferior of males, and her own easy access to learning made it difficult for her to understand the sense of deprivation "felt by middle- and lower-class women who put the right to an education high on their list of priorities as they developed their feminist program. In later life, Florence Nightingale dabbled in philosophical speculation as well as more practical affairs, and to test her ideas she regularly consulted with such intellectual giants of her time as John Stuart Mill, Benjamin Jowett, and the historian, J. A. Froude. That Florence Nightingale was an elitist, there is no denying.

W. E. N. certainly did not inspire Florence to go out into the world and serve humanity. Much like Joan of Arc, to whom she compared herself, Florence proclaimed that at crucial periods in her life God spoke to her, calling her to His service. She recorded that on February 7, 1837, God first called to her to serve Him.[3] But it was not till 1845 that she concluded the service He wanted her to perform was to care for the sick and disadvantaged.

During these years of inward struggle she played the dutiful daughter at home. Her mother had put her in charge of the pantry and the linen room, and she fulfilled her social obligations. She fully realized that at some point her own sense of mission would have to be revealed to her family, but she bided her time as she worked through her conflicts. Her mother and sister were no role models, but she found others. There was Mary Clarke (Clarky), who had escaped to Paris from the restricted life of Victorian England and became an influential political figure. It was to Mary Clarke that she complained of the "faddling, twiddling, and the endless tweedling of nosegays in jugs"[4] that constituted the life of a Victorian lady. She developed a "passion" for her cousin Marianne Nicholson. "I never loved but one person with passion in all my life, and that was her,"[5] she wrote in 1846. She was undoubtedly attracted by Marianne's musical gifts, but chiefly it was her self-confidence and daring that engaged Florence.

Florence Nightingale had a number of suitors, but the conflict over career and marriage did not seriously engulf her until she met Richard Monckton Milnes in 1842. At 33, Milnes had achieved great success in London society and had a promising political career. He was a poet of some talent but had a greater gift for discerning poetic genius in others. He was said to be witty, amiable, and kind. Florence was taken by him, especially with his humanitarianism and his inclination for philanthropic work. He loved children and worked for many years to improve the treatment of young criminals. Florence and Milnes had other things in common. Her birth in Italy and her travels had brought about a love of that country. Milnes had been brought up in Italy and "preserved Italian picturesqueness in his appearance and manners."[6]

During the summer of 1842, Milnes came to the Nightingale estate at Embly several times. He fell in love with Florence and made a stunning impression on Fanny, Parthe, and W. E. N., who treated him as one of the family and fully expected Florence to marry him.

Unbeknown to the rest of her family, 1842 was a crucial year for Florence in another way. She came closer to understanding her own goals for self-fulfillment. Conditions in what were known as the "hungry forties" affected her. The late 1830s saw the beginnings of a depression in England that lasted into most of the 1840s. By the summer of 1838, 50,000 workers were unemployed in Manchester alone. Poor harvests contributed to the general malaise, and starvation literally stared thousands in the face. Florence Nightingale was not unaware of the homeless and hungry wandering the countryside of Hampshire and Derbyshire and of her own position as one of the "idle rich."

Nightingale's friendship with Lord Anthony Ashley, the social reformer, provided some direction to her discontent. When he informed her of the abysmal conditions in the hospitals and poorhouses of England, she began to focus her energies on the subject matter that would occupy her for the rest of her life. She discovered that hospitals were places of degradation and squalor. The nurses, who came from the poorest classes, had a reputation for immorality and degeneracy. Supervision was almost totally lacking and therefore discipline was hard to maintain. Since they were overworked, piteously underpaid, constantly vulnerable to disease and assault, it was not a profession any respectable woman considered entering.

Through a chance remark, Florence learned of a hospital in Kaiserswerth, Germany where potential nurses could get training. By 1846, having determined that the service she was called upon to do was nursing, she apprehensively broached the idea to her family, asking permission to take nurse's training for three months at Salisbury, which was not too far from the Embly estate. Florence Nightingale's family could not have been more shocked had she proclaimed her desire to become a prostitute. A nine-year struggle ensued before the family finally relented. The initial reaction was consternation on the part of W. E. N., anger on the part of her mother, and hysterics bordering on a nervous breakdown from Parthe.

Parthe's reactions were the most difficult to deal with. Parthe had cast herself as the adoring, indispensable sister who did not want to be left out of any part of Florence's life. Having submerged her being in Florence, but having no taste whatsoever for Florence's ambitions, she was reduced to manipulating Florence to play her appointed role in Victorian society through attacks of hysteria and periodic nervous breakdowns whenever Florence threatened to take an independent path. Florence felt enormous guilt and despair — despair that caused her to consider converting to Catholicism and becoming a nun. Her final rejection in 1849 of a proposal from Richard Monckton Milnes — a decision she insisted she "agonized over" — was another blow to her family.

In 1850, Florence combined a trip to the Continent with a visit to Kaiserswerth, the hospital in Germany that gave training for nurses. She came home filled with enthusiasm only to find Parthe on the verge of another nervous breakdown. Her mother reproached her for her selfishness and irresponsibility and demanded that she devote the next six months to Parthe. She acceded but in retrospect described it as "an act of insanity."[7]

After three months of attending to Parthe and trying to blend into her life, Florence was actually contemplating suicide. She wrote, "My God, what will become of me? I have no desire but to die." She did not blame her sister for her demands, but merely reproached herself, and thus became deeply depressed. Continuous attempts to placate Parthe were fruitless. When she made plans to go back to Kaiserswerth for training, her attempt to conciliate Parthe was totally rebuffed. "My sister threw my bracelets which I offered her to wear in my face and the scene which followed was so violent that I fainted."[8]

Florence left for Kaiserswerth filled with guilt and continued to make overtures to her sister. She wrote of her happiness in the spartan conditions in which she lived; how she was mastering her training and was completely fulfilled and satisfied. "Give me your faith," she wrote Parthe, "Trust me . . . help me. Say to me, 'Follow the dictates of that spirit within thee' . . . My beloved people I cannot bear to grieve you. Give me your blessing."[9] Parthe never responded, and Florence never appealed to her again.

Instead Florence Nightingale poured out her anger at her sister and all she represented in *Cassandra*, a pamphlet she wrote in 1852 but that was not published till after her death. As a radical feminist critique of the repressed life of the Victorian middle- and upper-class woman, *Cassandra* has been ranked with John Stuart Mill's *The Subjection of Women* (1869) and adumbrates Virginia Woolf's *A Room of One's Own* (1929).

Nightingale makes clear in *Cassandra* ʼhat every feminist in the nineteenth century pointed out — that women were contingent beings who must fit their lives to the needs of others. "Women never have a half-hour in all their lives that they can call their own, without fear of offending or hurting someone else. Such a life must exclude any serious work or study, since the demands of either would make women unavailable to others. So women play through life — taking up one activity after another."[10]

She lamented, "Passion, intellect, moral activity — these three have never been satisfied in woman. In this cold and oppressive conventional atmosphere, they cannot be satisfied. To say more on this subject would be to enter into the whole history of society, of the present state of civilization."[11]

Nightingale expressed anger over the fact that women themselves accepted that they were to have no occupation of sufficient importance not to be interrupted except "suckling their fools." Women wrote books to support this view, and trained their children to observe it.

Nightingale noted that women's wasted energies find outlets in fantasies and daydreams, which she was haunted by herself, causing a great deal of anxiety. Woman's domestic duties were mere "high-sounding words." What are they? They include answering letters from friends, keeping herself sufficiently informed about the world to be amusing at breakfast, and driving in her carriage with visitors. She felt that all these activities led a woman to nothing of substance.

Florence Nightingale identified marriage and the family, the twin bulwarks of Victorian life, as the oppressors of women. She had no difficulty resisting marriage; it was the bonds of the family that imprisoned her. Her remarks on the family are scathing.

> The family? It is too narrow a field for the development of an immortal spirit, be that spirit male or female. The family uses people, *not* for what they are, not for what they are intended to be, but for what it wants them to be — for its own uses. It thinks of them not as what God has made them, but as the something it has arranged that they shall be. If it wants someone to sit in the drawing room, *that* someone is to be supplied by the family, though that member may be destined for science, or for education, or for active superintendence by God, i.e., by the gifts within . . . This system dooms some minds to incurable infancy [the way she thought of Parthe] others to silent misery [herself].[12]

Nightingale called on women to "Awake . . . all ye that sleep, Awake! The time is come when women must do something more than tend the 'domestic hearth.'"[13] For Cassandra it was too late. Suffocated by her family's demands, retreating into the despair of daydreams and fantasy, Cassandra dies. Nightingale resolved her conflict by killing the passive Cassandra ("Welcome, beautiful death!") but she heeded her own call to help others, to unshackle herself and live.

The writing of *Cassandra* converted despair to active rebellion. It confirmed her determination to live her own life, to become her own person. On another level it explains why Nightingale resisted becoming part of the women's movement in the nineteenth century. She had freed herself through an heroic act of will, which she asked other women to emulate. She never doubted that they could do so if they wished to.

In truth, Florence Nightingale was helped along the path to freedom by two crucial events. In 1853, her father became her ally and made her self-sufficient by settling an allowance of 400 pounds a year on her — a munificent sum at that time. Her release from Parthe was finally mandated by a physician with a shrewd knowledge of psychology. The separation was considered essential, not because of Florence Nightingale's desires for independence, but for Parthe's sake. After Parthe suffered another of her breakdowns, Sir James Clarke insisted Florence must separate herself from Parthe, since her sister's only chance of regaining mental balance was to learn to live without Florence and develop her own resources and her own identity. Nightingale's comment at this turn of events is filled with irony. She wrote ten years later: "A very successful physician once seriously told a sister who was being devoured that she must leave home in order that the Devouree might recover health and balance which had been lost in the process of devouring. This person being myself."[14] She described it as a terrible lesson that tore open her eyes as nothing else could have done.

In 1853, at the age of thirty-three, Florence Nightingale embarked on her chosen career of nursing. She assumed the duties of Superintendent of Hospital for Invalid Gentlewomen in Harley Street, London. In 1854 the Crimean War broke out between England, France, and Russia. When news of the frightening casualties came back to England, casualties caused more by disease than by bullets, Florence Nightingale followed her calling there and entered the pages of history. Her struggles to provide sanitary conditions, relief from overcrowding, decent food — some measure of comfort to the sick and dying — need no repetition here. They made her a national heroine when she returned to England in 1856. The esteem in which she was held could not have been higher.

Now Parthe and Fanny (her mother) welcomed her with open arms, seeking to bask in her reflected glory. Florence Nightingale had other ideas. Convinced because of illness contracted in the Crimea that there was little time left to her, she was determined to bring about reforms in the War Office that would make better sanitary conditions and the health of the soldiers a major priority. She was also determined to continue her nursing career. When Parthe and her mother made her work difficult by demanding that she accept the acclaim of a grateful nation, she turned herself into an invalid, to protect herself against this renewed invasion and to enable her to continue her work. Her invalidism has been called a "creative malady"[15] — a psychoneurosis that freed her from the presence and demands of her family. She had an "attack" every time Parthe threatened a visit, effectively turning the tables on her sister.

Parthe found her own fulfillment when she married Sir Henry Verney in 1858. At the time of the marriage, Parthe was close to 40; Verney was 56. It was his second marriage; her first. Verney had originally held a commission in the life guards and intended to make the military his career. But when he inherited the family estates in Buckinghamshire, he was so appalled by the miserable conditions of the land and the tenants that he decided to devote himself to becoming a model landlord. He became a pioneer in rural housing and administration. He drained and reclaimed land, built model cottages, and was active in the administration of the Poor Law. When cholera broke out in his district, Verney helped nurse the sick and subsequently collected funds to build a county hospital. He became Liberal member for Buckinghamshire in 1832 and held the seat for periods amounting to thirty-one years.

Verney's humanitarian endeavors brought him into contact with Florence to whom he had proposed in 1857, but she rejected him as she had rejected all her suitors. After this rebuff, he became attached to Parthe and asked her to marry him. We will never know how Parthe felt, but she accepted, and through the marriage Florence and her sister Parthe were reunited.

Florence emerged from her retirement and was a frequent visitor at the Verney estate, where she discussed the problems of establishing a nursing school, a long-treasured ambition, with both Verney and her sister. In 1860, with Parthe's encouragement, she established the Nightingale School and Home for Nurses at St. Thomas's Hospital, London, with capital from the Nightingale Fund which had been established in 1855.

She devoted a great deal of time and attention to its administration, conscious that she was opening an avenue for women to become independent and also serve humanity. She was providing the alternative to marriage and motherhood that she herself had chosen. She insisted nursing would become an honorable and respected profession only as nurses showed their dedication and commitment, their willingness to sacrifice.

For her part, Parthe became a successful and prominent hostess at the Verney estate, which was a center for political discourse. Her fulfillment in marriage brought out her suppressed creative side, and she began writing novels, one of which, *Lettice Lisle*, was published in 1865. She became the privileged guardian of her sister's shrine. After Verney's death, when Parthe became crippled by arthritis, Florence was her devoted nurse until her death in 1890. When Parthe truly needed her nursing skills, and was not dissembling with hysterical fits as she did during their younger days, Florence was only too glad to provide her with care and comfort to the end of her days.

It is clear that Florence and Parthenope Nightingale represented the opposite poles of nineteenth-century womanhood. Florence was rebellious against the conventions that the Victorian woman was supposed to uphold — that of the "angel in the house." Parthenope accepted these ideals wholeheartedly, from the endless social obligations to marriage as the ultimate goal of womanhood.

Florence lived on until 1910, scarcely aware that the women's movement was becoming violent on behalf of the suffrage. In the 1860s, when she was deeply immersed in her nursing school, an admirer, John Stuart Mill, appealed to the most beloved woman in England to lend her support to women's rights. Their correspondence from 1860 to 1867 reveals much about Nightingale's philosophy of feminism tempered by her experiences in her later years.

In 1860, Mill had asked Nightingale to support a movement enabling women to qualify as doctors on the same basis as men. Nineteenth-century feminists, much like those of the twentieth century, believed that women should not be excluded "by law or usage" from any field of endeavor. Mill was surprised when Nightingale questioned whether women should enter male dominated professions. Her experiences in the Crimea taught her that the male approach to medicine was impersonal, doctors usually treating their patients as numerous organs.

Florence Nightingale in fact typified the nineteenth-century view that women, innate nurturers, were more compassionate, more idealistic, and more moral than men. Women were the civilizers, the healers; men the destroyers, the warmongers who thought of human beings in abstract terms.[16] It was essential that women not emulate men as they entered the male-dominated world. According to a more contemporary view, women speak "in a different voice"[17] from that of men, and they should not change their tune.

Parthe had accused her sister of being more a man than a woman in her desire to enter the public world and have a career. Now Florence was turning that accusation against the women who wanted equality on male terms. She also undoubtedly resented the fact that she found so few supporters for her own priorities among the middle-class women's movement. She was particularly irked with women who "jawed" about gaining employment opportunities. She was providing employment opportunities for women in the nursing profession — a chance to buckle down and do humanitarian service that was considered by nineteenth-century standards to be women's special calling. There was a desperate need for qualified nurses. Nightingale complained, "We can't find them. They won't come."[18]

In retrospect, many of Florence Nightingale's doubts about the women's movement were well founded. She was skeptical that the suffrage would bring with it the reforms in education, employment opportunities, and equal pay that suffragists expected. In 1867 she was correct in her assessment that it would take a long time before women actually got the vote. According to all contemporary historians, the suffrage, when it finally was realized in the early twentieth century, was more a symbolic than substantive victory.

Florence Nightingale recognized that women should have choices. She became a reluctant supporter of the suffrage and eventually agreed that women should enter male professions. The current women's movement is being criticized because it has ignored and sometimes demeaned women who choose domesticity, home, and family as a way of life. That was Parthe's choice.

Florence chose a career. Eventually each came to appreciate the choice of the other.

## NOTES

1. See Lytton Strachey, *Eminent Victorians* (New York: G. P. Putnam's Sons, 1918).
2. Cecil Woodham Smith, *Florence Nightingale* (New York: McGraw Hill, 1951) p. 6.
3. Ibid., p. 12.
4. Ibid., p. 33.
5. Ibid., p. 33.
6. Ibid., p. 42.
7. Ibid., p. 98.
8. Ibid., p. 60.
9. Ibid., p. 62.
10. Florence Nightingale, *Cassandra*. Introduction by Myra Stark. (New York: The Feminist Press, 1979) p. 12.
11. Ibid., p. 29.
12. Ibid., p. 37.
13. Ibid., p. 13.
14. Smith, *Florence Nightingale*, p. 66.
15. Strachey, *Eminent Victorians*, p. 177.
16. For nineteenth-century views of the differing mentalities between men and women, see Sylvia Strauss, *"Traitors to the Masculine Cause": The Men's Campaigns for Women's Rights* (Westport, CT: Greenwood Press, 1982).
17. See Carol Gilligan, *In A Different Voice* (Cambridge: Harvard University Press, 1981).
18. Florence Nightingale, "The Faults of Women" (1862) in *Strong Minded Women*, edited by Janet Horowitz Murray. (New York: Pantheon Books, 1982).

# 7 Two Sisters Have I*
## Emily Dickinson's Vinnie & Susan

Adalaide Morris

*Reprinted from *The Massachusetts Review*, copyright 1981, The Massachusetts Review, Inc.

Susan Gilbert Dickinson

Lavinia Dickinson

Emily Dickinson

Sisterhood — that is, primary and bonding love from women — is, like motherhood, a capacity, not a destiny. It must be chosen, exercised by acts of will.
— Olga Broumas

Emily Dickinson had two sisters, one inherited and the other acquired. The
earliest was Vinnie: Lavinia Norcross Dickinson, born when Emily was two
years old. The second was Sue: Susan Gilbert Dickinson, appropriated as
friend when Emily was twenty, sanctioned as sister-in-law six years later. It
might be said that sisterhood was with Vinnie found and with Susan made,
yet it is important to emphasize that her bonding with both women was not
accidental but essential. It was, in Olga Broumas's term, "chosen": a capacity
developed through lifelong acts of desire and definition.

"It cannot be insisted too much," her biographer Richard Sewall reminds
us, "that, in Emily's limited circle, everyone counted."[1] The smallest circle
was the family: her mother, father, brother Austin, and Vinnie. Her mother
was unobtrusive, her father remote; Austin, though at first close, "married —
and," as Emily put it, "went East"[2] — three hundred yards east to his home
with Sue. That left Vinnie, Emily's enduring companion, and it annexed Sue,
Emily's lifelong fascination. Though the other members of her family signi-
fied, it was her sister and sister-in-law who provided a connection lasting until
death. The three women lived side by side for thirty years, exchanging bread,
fruit, and jellies, sharing news and books, suffering all the exaltations and
erosions of an intense daily life. Emily's bond with her sisters was eager, stub-
born, and solicitous. "Sisters are brittle things," she wrote. "God was penuri-
ous with me, which makes me shrewd with Him" (L, 353).

Her shrewdness is her effort to transform less into more. In this she uses
two means which characterize her art and life alike: compression and polarization. An essential quality of Dickinson's verse is what Robert Weisbuch calls
its "compressed inclusiveness": its narrow range combined with a seemingly
unbounded scope.[3] This paradoxical blend is achieved through a process of
analogy-making, the charging of details until they expand into symbols and
encompass a breadth beyond the range of the particular. This is in her poetry
the equivalent of the process in her life through which she deliberately nar-
rowed her circle in order to expand her horizon. "My friends are a very few,"
she wrote in her thirtieth year. "I can count them on my fingers — and besides,
have fingers to spare" (L, 366). Like a detail transformed into a symbol, each
friend, in her shrewdness, comes to represent a realm. They become, through

few, the dramatis personae of a crowded world, the plentitude which she called her "estate" (*L*, 338).

If compression is the stress Dickinson puts on a particular in order to charge it with significance, polarization is the distribution of charged particulars into patterns of opposition. "The complexity of [Dickinson's] mind," as Albert Gelpi notes, "is not the complexity of harmony but that of dissonance."[4] Her poetry reveals a temperament which insists on contradiction, paradox, and polarity. Each experience has two sides; each conception is held against an opposite; each personality is set beside its antitype. The characters who populate Dickinson's letters and poetry are, then, not only charged with symbolic significance but placed at poles from which they can enact dramas of division. The most exact and intimate of these dramas is the story of Dickinson's sisters: the clash of Vinnie and Sue.

In 1858 Dickinson wrote a poem which sets the terms, predicts the details, and appropriates the participants of this clash. It begins,

> One Sister have I in our house,
> And one, a hedge away.
> There's only one recorded,
> But both belong to me.
> (*P*, 14)

The first sister, Vinnie, recorded in the official prose of birth certificates and census lists, remained in the house all her life: we will see her representing the daily bustle of domesticity, the familiar, safe, and dutiful domain of the conventional woman. The sister-in-law, Sue, is recorded most vividly in private documents, in the intense letters and poems Dickinson sent across the lawn. Always "a hedge away," Sue represents for Emily the other pole of womanhood: the antidomestic woman, tempter, betrayer, narcissist, and visionary, the woman in touch with power, possessed of secret knowledge, dangerous, reviled, and perilously desired.

"'House' is being 'cleaned,'" Dickinson confided to a friend from the refuge of her room. "I prefer pestilence. That is more classic and less fell" (*L*, 453). "Fell": terrible, destructive, swift as a fell swoop—the hyperbole sets the tone for her portrait of Vinnie waging war with clutter. Vinnie enters the letters through a cloud of dust sweeping stairs (*L*, 193), "sewing away like a *fictitious* seamstress" (*L*, 175), making the garden (*L*, 406), training the honeysuckle (*L*, 410), trading with a tin peddler (*L*, 416), "cruis[ing] about to transact the commerce" (*L*, 311). In all the descriptions she is plucky and persistent. In some she seems as burdened as Atlas (*L*, 633), "far more hurried than Presidential Candidates . . . for *they*," Emily explains, "have only the care of the Union, but Vinnie the Universe" (*L*, 676).

Emily did what she termed "the Butterfly part" of the housekeeping; poor Vinnie did "the Moth part" (*L*, 924). Among other things this means that she bustles to protect what the Sermon on the Mount describes as "treasures upon earth, where moth and rust doth corrupt" (Matt. 6.19). Though Sue was reportedly such an intimidating housekeeper that her guests wiped their feet all the way up the walk,[5] to Emily she suggested not earthly but heavenly treasure, the kind neither moth nor rust can reach. To emphasize this, in drafting a late letter she borrowed the conclusion of the Sermon on the Mount's analogy: "where the treasure is," she assured Sue, "the heart is also" (*L*, 912).

Throughout her life, Dickinson chided her heart for idolatry of Sue. Where the descriptions of Vinnie are mock heroic, those of Sue tend to be reverent, frequently appropriating Biblical language, rhythms, and fervor. "'Eye hath not seen, nor ear heard, nor can the heart conceive' *my* Susie, whom I love" (*L*, 208), she writes, and one Sunday she conducts, in tandem with the pastor, her own service:

> when he said "Our Heavenly Father," I said "Oh Darling Sue"; when he read the 100th Psalm, I kept saying your precious letter all over to myself, and Susie, when they sang . . . I made up words and kept singing how I loved you, and you had gone. (*L*, 201)

Even allowing for playful self-mockery, Emily's stance toward Sue amounts to a kind of worship. "I have lived by this," she summarizes in the year after Sue's engagement. "It is the lingering emblem of the Heaven I once dreamed" (*L*, 306).

Sue stands, then, as an emblem for the heavenly, Vinnie represents the earthly: from these two premises derive the details of the mythology. Vinnie's power, for example, is local and temporal; Sue's is universal and eternal. Vinnie rules in the domain of the house, the garden, and the village shops through a combination of industriousness and cantankerousness. Her virtues render her "brave — faithful — punctual" (*L*, 676). As she fronts the merchants and fusses over the family, she seems to insure no less than the orderly progression of time: "When [Vinnie] is well," Emily sighs, "time leaps. When she is ill, he lags, or stops entirely" (*L*, 353).

Dickinson's descriptions of Sue, on the other hand, endow her with a Kingdom, Power, and Glory that transcend such matters as the leaping and stopping of time. "Be Sue — while I am Emily," she urges. "Be next — what you have ever been — Infinity — " (*L*, 830). "Cherish Power — dear," she exhorts. "Remember that stands in the Bible between the Kingdom and the Glory, because it is wilder than either of them" (*L*, 631). Again and again she reminds Sue that "Power is Glory, when it likes, and Dominion, too — " (*L*, 432). The obligation to be Power and Glory, if exhilarating, must also have been wearisome for Sue. Emily imposes it, in one way or another, on each of their transactions.

The power Emily attributes to Sue is not industry but enchantment. In the exuberant early letters Emily swears that the very words "Dear Susie" make the sun warm and the hills leave their work (*L*, 208). The mere promise of Sue's presence dots the sky with gold (*L*, 223) and fits Emily with "wings as white as snow, and as bright as the summer sunshine" (*L*, 216). Even in the troubled later years the magic persists, for "a Spell," as Emily reminds Sue, "cannot be tattered, and mended like a Coat—" (*L*, 673): it exists independent of time.

Other differences follow from these. While Vinnie's influence, for example, is always moral and benign, Sue's sometimes seems to Emily dangerous and immoral, a form of sorcery. Vinnie's limits make her a comic figure— "Vinnie thinks Vermont is in Asia" (*L*, 561); Vinnie admires the "Fruits of the Spirit" but if pushed "prefers Baldwins" (*L*, 840). Her simplicity, however, also makes her a trustworthy moral guide. "If she says I sin," Emily testifies, "I say, 'Father, I have sinned'—If she sanctions me, I am not afraid" (*L*, 348). Her upright common sense protects Emily.

The notes to Sue, in contrast, resonate with spiritual danger. "Susan knows she is a Siren—," Dickinson insists, "and that at a word from her, Emily would forfeit Righteousness" (*L*, 612). Bewitching, seductive, insidiously tempting, Sirens lure the susceptible to destruction, and Emily, it seems, was always susceptible to Sue. "I can defeat the rest," she laments late in life, "but you defeat me, Susan—" (*L*, 631).

Sue's appeal was composed of many things, among them contiguity, intellectual kinship, familial ties, and Susan's social charisma. Underlying all these, however, were two more essential bonds: passion and poetry. Vinnie all her life exerted a steadying influence; Sue always excited and disturbed Emily. In the nineteenth-century world they inhabited, an intense and sensuous intimacy between girls was expected and accepted, and Emily's early letters frequently mention the delights of handholding, hugs, and kisses.[6] Sometimes, however, the desire becomes more urgent and disruptive. In 1852, for example, Emily complains of sleeplessness and weeping: "I hope for you so much, and feel so eager for you, feel that I *cannot* wait, feel that *now* I must have you— . . . the expectation once more to see your face again, makes me feel hot and feverish, and my heart beats so fast" (*L*, 215). After Austin marries Sue and settles next door, the letters no longer request embraces, but they contain no less passion. The difference is that now they describe this passion as an element of Sue's character. Overwhelming, excessive, searing to those nearby, Sue is compared to "torrid Noons" (*L*, 831). She is "an Avalanche of Sun!" (*L*, 733), a "torrid Spirit!" (*L*, 791), a temptress from the *Arabian Nights* (*L*, 465).

The last description is telling, for part of Sue's attraction is that she shares with Emily a world of literary energy and allusion. When girls they took parts in Longfellow's *Kavanagh* (*L*, 102) and indulged in "Reveries" after the style of Ik Marvel (*L*, 144). As women they read and discussed such writers as George Eliot, Thomas à Kempis, Rebecca Harding Davis, and Disraeli. Emily sends Sue bits of literary jokes, news, and gossip. She dreams Sue meets Tennyson in a Boston publishing house (*L*, 455). So sure is she of their common fund, she sends Sue notes consisting wholly of brief quotations she expects Sue to recognize and apply. One, in its entirety, reads "'Egypt—thou knew'st'—" (*L*, 533). She could count on Sue to recall from *Anthony and Cleopatra* the rest of the speech:

> Egypt, thou knew'st too well,
> My heart was to thy rudder tied by the strings,
> And thou shouldst tow me after. O'er my spirit
> Thy full supremacy thou knew'st, and that
> Thy beck might from the bidding of the gods
> Command me. (III, xi, 56–61)

This is a game two avid readers might play, but it also suggests something more fundamental. Sue's complexities eventually became for Emily a text in themselves, one with disturbing implications about human nature. "With the exception of Shakespeare," Emily informed her, "you have told me of more knowledge than any one living—To say that sincerely is strange praise" (*L*, 733).

It is possible that Vinnie, herself an energetic reader,[7] knew more about Emily's gifts than has been supposed, but Emily's mythology relegates her to a world inventoried as "her duties, her pussies, and her posies" (*L*, 862). With Sue from the beginning Emily shared "the fancy that we are the only poets, and everyone else is *prose*" (*L*, 144). This accords exactly with the paradigm of the mythology. Poetry, when Dickinson defines it, is heavenly, universal, eternal, part of the Kingdom, the Power, and the Glory. It is dangerous and liberating, a wild force identified with passion and excess. "If I feel physically as if the top of my head were taken off," Dickinson summarizes, "I know *that* is poetry" (*L*, 474). Sue is everywhere associated with this force.

Vinnie's world is a prose world, and the portraits of Vinnie and her kittens (*L*, 559), Vinnie and the Fourth of July fire (*L*, 644), Vinnie "full of Wrath, and vicious as Saul" (*L*, 592) supply some of the finest examples of Dickinson's skill as a prose writer. She enters the poetry only once, in "One Sister have I," and then merely as a foil for Sue.

Susan's presence pervades the poetry. Johnson counts 276 poems sent to Sue,[8] and it is probable that many others, folded as if for insertion in envelopes, were exchanged with her. There are poems included with flowers, bread, and apples; holiday poems, vacation farewells, welcome home poems; poems on birthdays and poems on deaths. There are poems on Elizabeth Barrett Browning and George Eliot, on village characters, on family figures. There are poems of anger, playful poems, poems of love. Emily gave Sue drafts, redactions, and final copies, and there is at least one surviving example, certainly typical of many others, of Susan's response: an incisive, unintimidated critique of a draft of "Safe in their Alabaster Chambers" (*L*, 379–380). Sue saved each scrap of Emily's writing, pinned one poem to her sewing box (*P*, 1295), copied scores of others, forwarded at least one (*P*, 986) to an editor for publication, and read others eagerly to friends.[9] Without Sue, Emily would have lacked her most consistent audience and, from all appearances, her most intelligent and responsive critic.

One further function Sue served, however, is more fundamental than these. It is implied in an extravagant late note. "We remind [Susan] we love her," it begins. "Unimportant fact, though Dante did'nt think so, nor Swift, nor Mirabeau" (*L*, 509). In what way did Susan become for Emily what Beatrice was for Dante, Stella for Swift, Sophie for Mirabeau? Louise Bernikow, in her response to an essay contending that Dickinson's muse was a male father/ lover figure, suggests an answer. In the work of poets like Dickinson, Elizabeth Barrett Browning, Christina Rossetti, Edna St. Vincent Millay, and Sylvia Plath, she points out,

> a woman represents the "other" world, that of the imagination. Graves called the White Goddess "anti-domestic." The conflict in women between domesticity and antidomesticity, so clear in Plath, has something to do with the way women see our creativity, with the way we in fact imagine the muse. The struggle to free ourselves from the domestic often becomes our way of describing what it means to be inspired.[10]

Even accounting for hyperbole in Dickinson's statement, it remains true that Emily's obsession with Sue seems to have released her creativity. Sue, like Beatrice and Stella, empowered the poetry. It is for this reason that Susan's importance in Dickinson's work far exceeds any way we can account for it in terms of her place as confidante and critic. It isn't merely that Susan represents imagination. "Susan," in Dickinson's equation, "is Imagination" (*L*, 791).

Susan is also wife, mother, homemaker, and Amherst socialite, just as Vinnie was also reader, astringent commentator, and, in her own way, local eccentric. The important fact, however, is not the reality but the system that made Vinnie the domestic and Sue the antidomestic sister. They were not interchangeable. Dickinson, needing both, held them rigidly apart within her mythology. It is revealing that after Emily's death relations between Vinnie and Sue exploded: they struggled for Emily's manuscripts, they fought over Austin's affair with Mabel Todd, Vinnie accused Sue of cruelties which shortened Emily's life, and Sue set her dogs on Vinnie's cats.[11]

While Emily was alive, the triangle not only accommodated these divisions but thrived on the forces they generated. The apportioning of roles served many functions for Dickinson: it fixed definite poles in an otherwise uncertain world; it tied her firmly to both domestic and antidomestic realities; it provided both stability and excitement, shelter and inspiration; it exteriorized a tension which for many women remains debilitatingly interior; and, finally, it freed her to explore regions few have entered. Because Vinnie "buffet[ed] Life and Time" (*L*, 486) and Sue bodied forth imagination and eternity, Emily, held between them, could develop, in an unlikely era, her astonishing gifts.

## NOTES

1. *The Life of Emily Dickinson* (New York: Farrar, Straus and Giroux, 1974), I, 129.
2. *The Letters of Emily Dickinson*, ed. Thomas H. Johnson (Cambridge, Mass.: Harvard University Press, Belknap Press, 1958), II, 377. Further citations of *The Letters*, hereafter abbreviated as "*L*", will be documented in parentheses after the quotation. For ease of reference, I give the page number, not Johnson's letter number. Texts for the poems are from the edition by Thomas H. Johnson, *The Poems of Emily Dickinson*, 3 vols. (Cambridge, Mass.: Harvard University Press, Belknap Press, 1955), abbreviated here as "*P*". Poems will be cited by the number assigned them in the Johnson edition.
3. *Emily Dickinson's Poetry* (Chicago and London: University of Chicago Press, 1975), p. 11.
4. Albert Gelpi, *Emily Dickinson: The Mind of the Poet* (New York: Norton, 1965), p. 91.
5. Reported by David Peck Todd in an interview with Millicent Todd Bingham, in Sewall, *Life* I, 293.
6. Two excellent essays are helpful here: Carroll Smith-Rosenberg's "The Female World of Love and Ritual: Relations between Women in Nineteenth-Century America," *Signs* 1 (1975): 1–29, and Lillian Faderman's "Emily Dickinson's Letters to Sue Gilbert," *Massachusetts Review* 18 (1977): 197–225.
7. Although there is little evidence of this in Emily's letters, the entries from Vinnie's diary included in Jay Leyda's *The Years and Hours of Emily Dickinson*, 2 vols. (New Haven: Yale University Press, 1960), indicate she read seriously and steadily.
8. Johnson, *Poems*, III, 1197.
9. Recorded in an excerpt from Mabel Loomis Todd's journal, in Leyda, *Years and Hours*, II, 361.
10. "Comment on Joanne Feit Diehl's "'Come Slowly – Eden': An Exploration of Women Poets and Their Muse," *Signs* 4 (1978): 193–194.
11. For the details of this sorry time, see Sewall's explication of the "War between the Houses" (*Life*, I, Chs. 8–13, passim).

# 8 Billy Goat to Dolphin: Letters of Virginia Woolf to Her Sister, Vanessa Bell

Toni A. H. McNaron

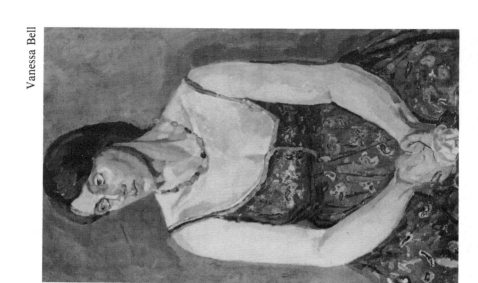

Vanessa Bell

Virginia Woolf

Montaigne once said that he made his books and his books made him. He was referring to his own essays, but I have applied his maxim to the books I've read, studied, taught, written about. Since historically such books have centered on male characters, I would have to say that my books unmade me; they oversimplified me, reduced me, confined me, eradicated me. From this invisible position, I was expected to conduct my life and my work. We understand by now that the act of reading and commenting upon women writers is one way to become visible, to make ourselves. Consequently, little confusion can arise over the fallacy of objectivity in critics or criticism. I read Virginia Woolf to find my selves and to find out about my selves. I write about her to validate that search and to share what I find with other women. For women are my audience now. If men read what I write, I am pleased, but I do not see their faces when I sit in my study.

Given my intense relationship to Virginia Woolf's life and words, I responded eagerly when a colleague asked if I'd be part of a panel on women writers and their blood sisters. I would naturally talk about Virginia and Vanessa. I recently read unpublished letters from Vanessa,[1] so I would talk about their personal relationship and about their responses to each other's work as artists. Reading Virginia's letters to her sister has made me keenly aware of the perils of doing radical feminist criticism — it often becomes inseparable from living a radical feminist life. I experienced increasing difficulty in sticking to my schedule. I spent some all-too-familiar time blaming myself for being lazy, a shoddy scholar, when suddenly I realized with a start that my work was too close to my life. I have spent many years working through the positive and negative consequences of growing up in a tightly closed family system. In that family, as in Virginia Stephen's, my mother was the focus of emotional energy. Like Virginia, I had an older sister, who I perceived as more attractive and better able to relate to and win the love of our mother than I. I now understand that much of my childhood and adolescence were fraught with situations in which I competed with my sister for many of the same things Virginia felt she lacked and Vanessa had — e.g., wit, charm, social grace, the requisite female attributes. I share these autobiographical similarities because I believe they both sharpen and deepen my insights into Virginia's life-long struggle to relate to Vanessa.

At present, I am in the process of disentangling my emotional ties to my sister. To read letter after letter in which Virginia wants something from

Vanessa that she is not getting, and to see that she knows that, has been pain-ful. I admire and identify with Virginia Woolf as much as with any writer I have read, any woman I have known. To see her cling to her sister, while cutting herself off from women who might have given to her largely, pas-sionately, and freely saddens and angers me. Once again, as in the case with her choice of critics,[2] Virginia was unable to let go of a person and a situa-tion in which she was doomed to see herself as lesser. The effect of hanging on to Vanessa in her daily life and her fictional portrayal of women has yet to be examined or even felt with anything like the degree of seriousness that it warrants. In this essay, I am opening that subject.

That Virginia saw herself as less than her sister shows up in the very names she gives them in the letters — Dolphin for Vanessa, Billy Goat for herself. If we must stop a moment to feel the different connotations for these two creatures, we can begin to understand the dynamic borne out in hundreds of letters. Dolphins are essentially graceful, playful, sensuous, at home in the female element, water. Billy goats are land-locked, gruff and crabby, often seen as chewing on such harsh substances as tin cans. In talking with a col-league about this essay, I was excited when she said that her first association with Billy Goat was scapegoat — a position in which Virginia put herself and allowed others, notably Vanessa, to put her. Personally, I think of dolphins as genderless or truly androgynous, while my images of billy goats have always been distinctly male. I think the most important associational contrasts for Virginia turn around gracefulness opposed to awkwardness, or lushness set against sparsity/harshness/limitation.[3]

Another evidence of Virginia's seeing herself as lesser is clear, since we now know that Vanessa lies behind the character of Katherine in *Night and Day*. This fact strongly suggests that Mary is then modeled on Virginia herself. Sud-denly the scene between them, when Mary sits fingering the hem of Katherine's soft skirt, takes on even more meaning than it already has for lesbian-feminist readers and critics.

As many of us women know from our own lives, the reality of a situation often cannot change our damaged perception of it. Such I think is the case with Virginia and Vanessa. Their letters reveal that Vanessa actually thought her sister the greater creative genius. She also saw her as more able to handle the affairs of daily life. Vanessa is constantly asking Virginia to get shoes or other provisions for her boys, to secure icing sugar or other foods tightly ra-tioned during the First World War. Repeatedly, letters reveal Vanessa ask-ing Virginia to do something about the problems of securing and retaining servants, a field of domestic activity in which Vanessa kept herself appallingly inept. Virginia does it all with calm, efficiency, and even gratitude to her sister for asking her to help. When Vanessa bungled matters that were already solved and then tried to blame Virginia, rarely do we see Virginia letting herself feel the anger that must have been there. If she speaks of such incidents at all, she talks of being hurt or surprised at her sister's anger. As someone who has often victimized myself, denying my own feelings in order to retain a spurious connection, I recognize what Virginia is doing all too clearly.

I see her making herself lesser in virtually every letter in which she asks to visit Vanessa or have Vanessa visit her. In these repeated, often brief phrases, I find the kernel of their relationship. One example will illustrate:

> Shall I come to tea on Thursday, that is tomorrow? Friday seems doubtful, so this is your only chance. Unless stopped I will come — but don't put yourself out, as I may even so be prevented. (*The Letters*, Vol. II, p. 537)

Eagerness and urgency are checked by self-sabotage. This tension runs through every invitation, and there are hundreds of invitations in the first four volumes of Virginia's letters. Her preference would have been to see her sister daily and, barring that, to write her and receive a letter. When they were apart, she often did write virtually every day, though her letters make clear that she heard very seldom from Vanessa, usually off in some sunny place with Duncan Grant, having a grand time while Virginia kept the two boys happy and their sisterly relationship intact. When they lived close by, Virginia wrote several times a week to say she could bike or walk over for lunch and tea or tea and dinner or dinner and the night, only to take it back by guessing that Vanessa was already too busy with guests or the baby or her art or Duncan — anything and anyone but her sister. This is a classic one-down behavior: assume the desired person will say no, then say it for them, thereby softening the blow of rejection[4] and preserving the image of the desired as capable of no wrong.

Virginia was protecting herself from her sister and from her own deep disappointment and jealousy if Vanessa indeed wrote that she was too busy. I see her maintaining this one-down position in spite of the actual relationship between them. While older and attributed with superior knowledge and wisdom, Vanessa depended upon Virginia to take care of her. By inverting the expected nurturing roles, she established a profoundly unsettling structure. Virginia discounted herself and felt discounted, while simultaneously being cast as the responsible, competent manager of details and emotions. One symptom of an incestuous family system is precisely such inversions of nurturance behaviors: a young child is asked, usually covertly, by a parent or older sibling, to take care of them, when by all rights she or he should be being taken care of. These inversions are inappropriate and damaging, making it unduly hard for the child to feel deserving of basic human consideration and love. I believe the more we learn of Virginia's place in her family and of her feelings for her mother as well as for Vanessa, the closer we will come to understanding her and the central characters in her books.

By her own admission, Virginia's relationship to her sister was emotionally incestuous. Rather than arguing this point, I prefer to let Virginia present her own evidence. The following quotations come from the first four volumes of published letters or from manuscript letters written in the late thirties, which reflect how the sisters were relating late in Virginia's life. Quotations are in simple chronological order.

(To Violet Dickinson shortly after Vanessa's marriage to Clive Bell): I did not see Nessa, alone, but I realise that that is all over, and I shall never see her alone any more; and Clive is a new part of her, which I must learn to accept. Still . . . I can make a living out of what is left; and it is the purest of all earthly affections. (*The Letters*, Vol. I, p. 276)

(To Clive Bell about Vanessa's name): It contains all the beauty of the sky, and the melancholy of the sea, and the laughter of the Dolphins in its circumference, first in the mystic Van, spread like a mirror of grey glass to Heaven. Next in the swishing tail of its successive esses, and finally in the grave pause and suspension of the ultimate [sic] A breathing peace like the respiration of Earth itself. (*The Letters*, Vol. I, p. 282)

I shall probably weep when I leave you tomorrow evening, for more than a fortnight . . . shall you kiss me tomorrow? Yes, yes, yes. Ah, I cannot bear being without you. I was thinking today of my greatest happiness, a walk along a cliff by the sea and you at the end of it. (*The Letters*, Vol. I, pp. 354–355)

. . . oh, I long for you! There are bullocks here, with eyes like yours, and beautiful trembling nostrils . . . there's no doubt I love you better than anyone in the world! I don't think I am selfish about you. (*The Letters*, Vol. I, p. 406)

I should point out to you, that it is very dangerous to allow these animals* to go long cared for: they are apt to return to their savage ways. At present, I must confess, I never saw a more engaging troop: their fur is in excellent condition—teeth white, and lips inviting. They gibber if I only say 'Maria' (Vanessa) to them. I think you would be touched. No one kisses them here. (*The Letters*, Vol. I, pp. 409–410) [*Virginia called herself 'Apes' and 'Singe' often when she wished to be sensual with Vanessa. This passage refers to these 'animals.']

This haste explains the dulness [sic] of this letter: nevertheless every word glows like a horseshoe on the anvil with passion. These June nights! — how amorous they make one. Tell me how you are . . . (*The Letters*, Vol. I, p. 466)

It was a vision of pleasure to see you; I've thought of you 50 times each day— in fact you may be said to be a kind of running bass . . . I do adore thee. (*The Letters*, Vol. II, p. 51)

If I stay with you, shall I get special attention? petting and free rights of kissing and stroking the ladies mile.* Eh? (*The Letters*, Vol. II, p. 105) [*'ladies mile' refers to the inner arm, between wrist and elbow.]

We ought to be walking up and down making our winter plans now, but I suppose you dont [sic] want me as much as I want you. (*The Letters*, Vol. II, p. 112)

How pleasant it would be to see you here, or to roll on the downs together, and the Ape would steal kisses from the most secluded parts! (*The Letters*, Vol. II, p. 124)

Nothing would please me better than a letter every day in your roughly eloquent style. Even the handwriting has the quality of a great sheep dogs paw — a sheep dog which has been trotting sagaciously through the mud after its lambs all day long —. (*The Letters*, Vol. II, p. 298)

When I'm old, when Julian and Quentin and Angelica are out in the world, do let us become travelling matrons, and go round the provinces together, in handsome style, having buried our husbands, for I think its best to be a widow (I mean in a hotel —). (*The Letters*, Vol. II, pp. 458–459)

Well, so you have arrived (at St. Tropez). The vision of large hats against a translucent sea and the white legs of prostitutes is I admit very attractive; oh and the butterflies: how they make my mouth water — the apollos, the white admirals, the Sulphurs, the purple emperors; and Dolphin sitting on a terrace in flowered muslin drinking coffee out of a glass, and first dipping an oblong piece of sugar in the coffee and nibbling the brown bit. (*The Letters*, Vol. II, p. 486)

I often wake in the night and cry aloud Nessa! Nessa! Doesn't that comfort you? Well, not much, you say. (*The Letters*, Vol. II, p. 543)

You are a scandal to sisterhood not to have written — Everything in the way of affection is always left to me. The time will come when exhausted nature sleeps. But, you will say, the pen is lost; but, I reply, my stack of pens will only last, with care, 6 years. (*The Letters*, Vol. III, p. 255)

Vita is now arriving to spend 2 nights with me — L. is going back. I say no more; as you are bored by Vita, bored by love, bored by me, and everything to do with me, except Quentin and Angelica; but such has long been my fate, and it is better to meet it open eyed. Still, the June nights are long and warm; the roses flowering; and the garden full of lust and bees, mingling in the asparagus beds. I must go in and tidy up. (*The Letters*, Vol. III, p. 275)

Ever since I left Cassis I have thought of you as a bowl of golden water which brims but never overflows. (*The Letters*, Vol. III, p. 363)

I'm in a terrible state of pleasure that you should think Mrs. Ramsay so like mother. At the same time, it is a psychological mystery why she should be: how a child could know about her; except that she has always haunted me, partly, I suppose, her beauty; and then dying at that moment, I suppose she cut a great figure on one's mind when it was just awake, and had not any experience of life — Only then one would have suspected that one had made up a sham — an ideal. Probably there is a great deal of you in Mrs. Ramsay; though, in fact, I think you and mother are very different in my mind. (*The Letters*, Vol. III, p. 383)

I am very excited, partly at the thought of seeing you again. I am like a sea anemone which has had to keep all its tentacles curled up, and when its put in water (i.e, Dolphin) they come out and wave and tumble and are of an exquisite and incredible beauty: but Lord. Dolphin bites; or she squirts acid: Dolphin cant [sic] be depended on for more than 2 seconds — Dolphins a heartless brute. (*The Letters*, Vol. III, p. 478)

Indeed I am getting very wizend and dry without you. (*The Letters*, Vol. III, p. 494)

I am feeling extremely barren and dry without you — Angelica* will be a small shower of rain; but not enough — What happens when you leave me too long is that I go gadding wherever I'm asked and finally end in a rage of misery at my kind. (*The Letters*, Vol. III, p. 501) [*Angelica is Vanessa's daughter.]

I have quarrelled with many people because of my bad manners; calling them wrong names by mistake, so you must take me to your arms and cover me with kisses — . (*The Letters*, Vol. III, p. 509)

But with you I am deeply, passionately, unrequitedly in love — and thank goodness your beauty is ruined, for my incestuous feeling may then be cooled — yet it has survived a century of indifference. (*The Letters*, Vol. III, pp. 546–547)

I wish dolphin were by my side, in a bath, bright blue, with her tail curled. But then I've always been in love with her since I was a green eyed brat under the nursery table and so shall remain in my extreme senility. . . . My love has always been fuller than your thimble. (Manuscript of letter, Summer, 1937, Berg Collection, NY Public Library)

I rather think I'm more nearly attached to you than sisters should be. Why is it I never stop thinking of you, even when walking on the marsh this afternoon. . . . If you notice a dancing light on the water, that is me. The light kisses your nose, then your eyes, and you can't rub it off; my darling honey how I adore you and lord knows I can't say what it means to me to come into the room and find you sitting there. (Manuscript of letter, August 17, 1937, Berg Collection, NY Public Library)

I feel a lost old crone without you all; you can't think how I depend upon you and when you're not there the colour goes out of life, as water from a sponge; and I merely exist, dry and dusty. (Manuscript of letter, October 2, 1937, Berg Collection, NY Public Library)[5]

Given this intensity of feeling, Virginia must have felt particularly betrayed when Vanessa supported Leonard's theories of what was best for her during periods of mental strain. Vanessa helped Leonard force feed Virginia when she was ill, a program that terrified Virginia. She believed that if she ate in the prescribed quantities she would lose her abilities to write cleanly and powerfully, that physical flab created intellectual flab. Not to have her sister, toward whom she felt such fierce love and devotion, believe that she knew how to mend herself better than the inept psychiatrists or even her nurse-maid husband must have caused her much anguish.[6]

For Vanessa's part, her letters are much more grounded in the everyday: her household and children, the prolonged servant problem, her travels, her and Duncan's routines. Her letters often request Virginia to do some errand, as stated earlier. On rare occasions, she drops an intimate remark: "Please write for your letters are essential to life" (1926)[7]; "I expect you and I are in telepathic touch with each other as I have often thought. I had felt sure you had a headache before your letter came. . . . " (1928); "You do know really dont you how much you help me—I cant [sic] show it and I feel so stupid and such a wet blanket often but I couldn't get on at all if it weren't for you— so you mustn't mind my being or seeming so grumpy—I really oughtnt [sic] to see outsiders yet, I'm so incompetent at dealing with them" (1938).

From my own experience, I know that intermittent avowals keep me loyal within a relationship, while the other person continues to encourage me to perform my intended function. Given her view of herself as lesser than her sister, such periodic statements from Vanessa carried disproportionate weight for Virginia. Once she even went so far as to express her joy at receiving a kind word from Vanessa in terms of feeling like a puppy going around the house all day with a bone.

These sisters continued to correspond throughout Virginia's life, and she was true to her own predictions: She did remain in love with her sister, never getting directly angry at her, though occasionally being brave enough to write in a coyly miffed tone. Her relationship with Vanessa, admittedly "incestuous," blatantly sensual and desirous of intimacy, strangely unrequited and unrequitable, deserves our serious attention. It seems at least as important in assessing Virginia's adult sexuality to focus on this life-long entanglement as on the episodes with her step-brothers, George and Gerald Duckworth. I disagree with Quentin Bell on this matter. Being male himself, he would understandably have us believe that those Sunday afternoons and late nights, when these two males sexually abused their two half-sisters, were the cause of Virginia's sexual coldness. First of all, I do not find her "cold" sexually: reserved, even frightened, but who can read her prose and not respond to the pervasive sensuality of diction and metaphor in passage after passage? Surely we can trust her own remarks about George and Gerald, whom she seems to have found mildly amusing at times, certainly shallow, often bores. While in no way minimizing the effects on her as a child and young woman of being sexually abused by a male family member, I am asserting that the focus of Virginia Stephen Woolf's sexual energies was always women, and so it is crucial to look at her feelings toward her mother and her sister as the first women in her life. From her letters I am prepared to say that she never fully separated from her sister. As a result she remained ambivalent at best about intimacy with other women. Significantly enough, she seems often to have chosen for her closest friends women with whom it was easy for her to cast herself as lesser: younger than, less beautiful than, less talented than, less passionate than. I think immediately of her mother, Violet Dickinson, Vanessa, Vita Sackville-West, Ethel Smythe.

Her psyche kept her from feeling equal with women, while her society kept her from feeling equal with men. To allow this remark its full weight is to begin to feel the depth of isolation with which Virginia dealt throughout her life. Once I've done that, I am in a better place to assess her life and the books she struggled to write, often against fierce odds, always against the expected grain.

Only in the context of their work can Virginia ever see herself as equal to her sister. Vanessa and Virginia were vastly important to each other when it came to their art, though even here, they could create barriers to letting themselves speak with a full voice or be fully heard. At crucial points, each says that what the other thinks and feels about a painting or novel is the most important response she will get. At the end of Volume III of Virginia's letters we can read Vanessa's precious response to *To the Lighthouse*. This letter confirmed for Virginia in ways no other review or critique ever could that her characters had life and evocative powers, that she had succeeded. Vanessa's response to *The Waves* was similarly important, since in that book the death of Percival is Virginia's working out her own feelings about her brother Thoby's untimely death. In a letter written right after Virginia finished the manuscript, Vanessa speaks of being "submerged . . . left rather gasping, out of breathe [sic], choking, half-drowned. . . . " (Manuscript of letter, October 11, 1931, Berg Collection, NY Public Library). Later she makes one of her rare reciprocal statements to her sister, acknowledging both their lives as artists:

> Will it seem to you absurd or conceited or will you understand at all what I mean if I tell you that I've been working hard lately at an absurd great picture I've been painting off and on the last 2 years—and if I could only do what I want to—but I can't—it seems to me it would have some sort of meaning analogous to what you've done.

On her side, Virginia speaks often to Vanessa about a single painting or a show, almost always qualifying her remarks by saying she doesn't know how to discuss art. I want to share two instances, however, because they seem central. The first is from a March 1927 letter:

> All your pictures are built up of flying phrases. This is to me a very exciting and congenial stage. They have an air of complete spontaneity. The downs seem to billow; yet the hay cart is perfectly substantial. I daresay your problem will now be to buttress up this lyricism with solidity. I pronounce no opinion on that. I think we are now at the same point: both mistresses of our medium as never before: both therefore confronted with entirely new problems of structure. Of course your colour intrigues me, seduces, and satisfies me exquisitely. . . . I should like you to paint a large, large picture; where everything would be brought perfectly firmly together, yet all half flying off the canvas in rapture. (*The Letters*, Vol. III, p. 341)

Here Virginia lets them be equals if only for a few phrases. Additionally, she suggests future direction for Vanessa's work—something she hardly ever did. Since we know that Vanessa did attempt larger canvasses, we may see Virginia as being a genuine influence.

The other example of Virginia's close tie to her sister as artist appears in a letter of June 1938. She says: "The picture has just been nailed up—its perfectly lovely—firm as marble and ravishing as a rainbow. How I wish I were a painter" (Manuscript letter, June 1938, Berg Collection, NY Public Library). Her description indicates that she sees Vanessa as having achieved what she thought to be her challenge—buttressing lyricism with solidity ("marble" and "rainbow"). Virginia's ability to paint scenes belies her wish here and surely comes from her intimate association with her sister's work, and not merely from friends in Bloomsbury. So the debt is considerable on both sides.

Like many an artist, Virginia wrestled with the paradox of needing the excitement and stimulation of talking and being with people while knowing that precisely such stimulation drained off energy essential for creativity. Feeling this paradox, she needed to retain some sources outside herself who could evoke passionate feelings and phrases within her. Vanessa may well have been a relatively safe repository for Virginia's passionate fantasies. Certainly the letters are laced with the language of passion and desire. Given the heavy social taboo against incest, Virginia was not likely to act on her feelings for her sister, though we do not know this. What we do know comes from Virginia's own pen: she speaks of intimate physical contact with her sister in the most explicit terms.[8]

At some subconscious level, then, Vanessa becomes an outlet for heightened feeling expressed in highly charged erotic tones. In a wry way, it may have been more constructive for Virginia to pine away for an unrequitable love for her sister than to pursue some of the women with whom she might well have been sexually intimate. She also had Vita's example before her, since that lady let her actions follow her feelings in a most extravagant fashion. Since Virginia was convinced that Vita's writing was less focused than it might be and that it suffered from stylistic looseness, she may well have linked romantic behavior with weaknesses as a writer.

Many current readers will acknowledge the highly sensual language in which Virginia described nature and meetings or feelings between people. This fairly recent fact represents an improvement over former responses to her fictional creations as sexless—perhaps because her characters do not copulate as such. These same readers recognize the sparsity of explicit sexual experiences in Virginia's life, though her letters are making clear that she did have sexual contact with Vita, a long-debated issue important to Virginia's knowing her own female sexuality. We know from Bell's quoted sources that she and Leonard had almost no sexual exchanges, and we know from Virginia's own writings that she found the entire male atmosphere offensive. Given all this, critics puzzle over the discrepancy between direct, lived events and metaphoric handling of feelings. I see the letters to Vanessa as the missing link.

Rather than thinning her energies in a series of sexual relationships, Virginia chose to focus her passion and desire on a supposedly unobtainable object, who seems never to have asked her to stop writing in such sensual terms. It is too soon to say what mutual needs of these sisters were being met by this process, but it is not too soon to assert that by remaining in love with Vanessa, Virginia remained in touch with her own primal sensual and sexual feelings. Further, by writing her sister as often and for as long as she did, she gave herself a forum for phrasing those feelings in language that could then find its way into novel after novel. This may be the most significant way in which Vanessa nurtured Virginia's art—by allowing herself to be adored and, indeed, by asking for that adoration. I believe Virginia gained specifically in relation to style within her novels from this otherwise unequally fulfilled relationship with Vanessa.

From a letter written in June 1926 comes this poignant passage, remarking on her visit to Vanessa's current show: "I mean, people will say, What a gifted couple! Well: it would have been nicer had they said; Virginia had all the gifts; dear old Nessa was a domestic character—Alas, alas, they'll never say that now" (*The Letters*, Vol. III, p. 271). Virginia's ambivalence runs deep here, with her reference to her and her sister as a couple jostling her complicated wish to be the more talented of the two in some endeavor. She never resolved that ambivalence.

## NOTES

1. I read these letters while working at the Berg Collection on the correspondence between May Sarton and Louise Bogan. In my last week there, I could not resist holding pieces of paper which Virginia had held. Once reading her, I was intuitively drawn to her sister's letters: following that intuition has been important to me.

2. Though a thoroughly radical feminist, able to tell other women to look beyond patriarchs for support, Virginia was herself unable to give up her belief that men were more trustworthy as critics of her writing than women were.

3. Distinctly sexual connotations come into play when Virginia extends her use of "dolphin" to Vita Sackville-West. She does this in letters written from the summer of 1927 into the spring of 1928, a time when Virginia was feeling intensely jealous of Vita's growing restlessness to be falling in love with someone new. The clearest object of Virginia's anxiety was Dorothy Wellesley. Suddenly, she begins to refer to Vita as a dolphin acting in an oyster bed, an image carrying heavy vaginal overtones. This use of language with overtly sexual association confirms Virginia's depth of feeling and dramatizes her pained response to Vita's roving eye.

Calling her lover the same name otherwise reserved for her sister complicates even further Virginia's incestuous feelings for her sister. In looking at the many letters to Vanessa written during this same period, I am struck by the total absence of "Dolphin" in any of the addresses. Aside from this change the letters continue to be filled with verbal intimacies and pleas for special attention.

I am grateful to Yarrow Morgan, a lesbian/feminist critic and writer, for drawing this congruence to my attention after reading a draft of this essay.

4. Amidst this constant inviting and uninviting, this pleading for more letters, lapses occur. Months go by during which no letters or the merest business notes are sent to Vanessa. It is premature to speculate on what caused these, but I assume that when all her private writing is published, we can piece together scenes preceding such spells. We can then perhaps know whether Virginia periodically reached the limits of her patience with Vanessa or whether she tried at times to separate from her. Perhaps we will have to conclude that no psychological motivation exists at all. In any event, it will be a relief to have a view on this, since at present the lapses seem mostly odd and teasing. For instance, Volume IV of her letters contains both fewer and cooler letters to Vanessa. Simultaneously, this volume is full of letters to Ethel Smythe, with whom Virginia became extremely close during this time. Her letters to Ethel were answered in kind. In fact, for once Virginia found herself with someone who paid more attention to her than she wished. Consequently, she had the experience of setting boundaries on this relationship and of feeling overwhelmed by so much energy coming her way so intensely. I would wonder if these two observable facts are not causally related.

5. These quotations are representative and in no way exhaustive. I say this so readers can comprehend the depth and extent of the passionate feelings Virginia carried with her always for her sister.

6. For a fuller description of Vanessa's part in such "cures," see Roger Poole in *The Unknown Virginia Woolf* (Cambridge University Press, 1978), pp. 127–166.

7. This and the next two quotations come from manuscript letters held at the Berg Collection. The exact dates are May 27, 1926; February 2, 1928; February 4, 1938.

8. I am impressed by the relative ease with which Virginia spoke about her relations with her half-brothers. We know from letters that she talked about her experiences with her old Greek teacher, Janet Case. Even more amazing, we know from *Moments of Being* that she could talk about George and Gerald at meetings of her Memoir Club, the membership of which was preponderantly male. Incest victims usually feel a primary pressure against speaking about what has happened to them. Therefore, Virginia's ability to articulate her sexual abuse is radical. Furthermore, we also know from her own words that she wrote *To the Lighthouse* specifically to face her parents and write them out of her consciousness so that she could live and work without their spectres hanging over her. To then notice her silence about the nature of her relationship with Vanessa and its effects on her is to notice something significant. I think we can all admit that the sexual fantasies and emotional bonds that we talk about last or never are those that confuse, frighten and excite us the most. So Virginia's silence may be the loudest evidence that this relationship was the most central one in her adult life.

# 9 "She Is The One You Call Sister": Levertov's and Rich's Poems on Sisterhood

Robin Riley Fast

TSB-H

Denise Levertov and Adrienne Rich, while they might be considered opposites in some respects, share an appreciation of the sensuous, a recognition of the political nature of individual experience and of poetry, and the fact that each has written of her relationship with her sister, exploring movingly both the personal and the political importance of the relationship.

Levertov writes of the sister bond in a formal sequence; Rich, in poems that have appeared in several books over a period of years. Each examines a complex and changing bond, colored with rivalry and intimacy, loss and reaffirmation, shaped by forces inside each sister and outside both. They deal with similar dilemmas: each must recognize both her likeness to and difference from her sister. For each, the recognition of similarity and difference complicates a common double image, that of the sister as a mirror, or as "what I might have been."

Having confronted the difficulties of sisterhood, they suggest ways of moving toward relationships that may be both personally and politically sustaining. Understanding her sister and their relationship allows each poet to understand herself and to grow poetically and politically: Levertov becomes a more politically assertive writer, and Rich establishes a concrete bridge to relationships with other women. For both, then, their poems about their sisters contribute to the development of their poetry. And the fact that, in spite of their differences, Levertov's and Rich's responses to this topic have much in common suggests the truth of their findings for other sisters.

In her "Olga Poems," Denise Levertov explores and recreates her relationship with her dead sister, Olga. The primary fact of this relationship, as it is initially described, is distance.

> By the gas-fire, kneeling
> to undress,
> scorching luxuriously, raking
> her nails over olive sides, the red
> waistband ring —
>
> (And the little sister
> beady-eyed in the bed —
> or drowsy, was I? My head
> a camera —)
>
> Sixteen. Her breasts
> round, round, and
> dark-nippled —
>          (*Sorrow Dance*, p. 53)[1]

Olga, at 16, was sensuously alive; Denise was separated from her by years and experience. The sisters' present separation by death seems to confirm the earlier distance. The gap persists as the second poem describes Olga's nagging voice and chewed nails, symptoms of her rage at the world, a rage her younger sister did not share:

> What rage
>
> and human shame swept you
> when you were nine and saw
> the Ley Street houses,
> grasping their meaning as *slum.*
>           (*Sorrow Dance*, p. 54)

Denise, at nine, teased her sister about the slum, "admiring/architectural probity, circa/eighteen-fifty." Yet as poem ii ends, the adult Denise recognizes the paradox and contradiction at Olga's center: "Black one, black one,/there was a white candle in your heart." Paradox and contradiction, we will find, are characteristic of the sisters' relationship and essential to the reconciliation that Denise achieves through these poems.

Recurrent images and motifs suggest Olga's powerful character and the difficulties of the relationship. Images associated with fire indicate Olga's passionate anger, desire, and nonconformity. After Olga has cast off her family and disappeared, Denise dreams of her "haggard and rouged/lit by the flare/from an eel- or cockle-stand on a slum street" (p. 56). When she lies dying, her sister remarks that Olga's hatreds, her "disasters bred of love," and all history have "burned out, down/to the sick bone" (p. 57). The color black also recurs, suggesting the anguish of this black-haired, olive-skinned sister. Olga's desperate fury seems compelled by a vision expressed in her compulsively repeated "*Everything flows*" and in the image of "the rolling dark oncoming river" whose course she struggles to change: "pressing on/to manipulate lives to disaster . . . To change,/to change the course of the river!" (p. 55). The gradual transformation of these images, as the sequence develops, indicates the transformation of Denise's vision of Olga and their relationship.

The intensity of Denise's feelings and of her desire for reconciliation is evident in her tendency to repeat key words and phrases — Olga is "Ridden, ridden," or "Black one, black one" — and most powerfully in the poem immediately preceding the "Olga" sequence in *The Sorrow Dance*, "A Lamentation" (p. 52):

> Grief, have I denied thee?
> Grief, I have denied thee.
>
> That robe or tunic, black gauze
> over black and silver my sister wore
> to dance *Sorrow*, hung so long

in my closet. I never tried it on.

. . . . . . . . .

*Grief,*

*have I denied thee? Denied thee.*

But her grief and desire are mixed with uncertainty: fire burns, Olga's efforts to stem the flow are worse than useless, and she betrays her "blackness" when she dyes her hair blond. The younger sister's ambivalence is evident, too, as she vacillates between speaking to Olga and describing her in the third person, before she finally commits herself to sustained direct address, which carries her into a closer bond with Olga.

The sisters' estrangement seems to have several sources, which vary in importance over time. The poet repeatedly draws attention to the nine years' difference in their ages by referring to herself as "little sister," sitting in her "Littlest Bear's" armchair or riding her bike. The younger girl apparently resisted growing up and probably resented Olga's womanly body. But more than age separates them; their views of life are radically different. Olga seems to see life and history as relentlessly surging onward, carrying everything implacably toward disaster: "everything flows."[2] Her dominant impulse appears to be resistance. And her resistance takes the form of rage that "burns" but doesn't accomplish the change she desires, rage equivalent perhaps to that of Sylvia Plath, or to the "bomb" whose power Emily Dickinson managed only with great effort and skill to control. Bent on changing the world, Olga attempts to control her sister, who becomes one of the "human puppets . . . stung into alien semblances by the lash of her will" (p. 54). Her passion makes her overbearing, manipulative, and demanding — not the easiest person to love.

Denise, on the other hand, "feels" life as "unfolding, not flowing" (p. 56). Unlike the overwhelming river-like "flow" against which Olga struggles, "unfolding" suggests the opening of a plant — that is, life, and the power of individual life. It implies the quiet process of gradual growth and assurance about the continuity and the essential goodness of life. "Unfolding" is thus, at least in this context, more consistent with the organicism that moves most of Levertov's poetry. Her different view of life gives Denise a different mode of action and thought. She is careful, quiet, controlled. Early in her assessment of Olga and their relationship, this habit sometimes makes for cool, unsympathetic distance, as evidenced in her nine-year-old response to the slums. However, this quiet mode helps her gradually to reconnect with Olga, for it enables her to balance and examine multiple layers of experience in long, complex lines that move surely, if not rapidly, to the final, affirming image of Olga.

Beneath the (at first apparently absolute) estrangement, the poet reveals an impulse to reach out to her sister, to understand, and recover the bonds between them. It is an impulse based in implicit acknowledgment of shared experience and love. Her desire for connection is most evident when she evokes moments of intimacy, often rediscovered beneath the surfaces of the same words, events, or scenes that estrange the sisters, indicating that their bond preceded, and must finally bridge, the distance between them. Thus, Denise twice recalls Olga's loneliness, only to be reminded of their deep bond:

> . . . you went walking
> the year you were most alone
>
> . . . . . . . .
> crossing the ploughlands (whose color I named *murple*,
> a shade between mauve and brown that we loved
> when I was a child and you
> not much more than a child)
> . . . . . . . .
>
> How many books
> you read in your silent lodgings that winter,
> how the plovers transpierced your solitude out of doors with
> their strange cries
> I had flung my arms to in longing, once by your side
> stumbling over the furrows —
> *(Sorrow Dance*, pp. 58–59)

Recalling what they have shared, the poet first emphasizes the similarity, not the difference, in their ages, and then, as she sees herself flinging open her arms in longing, acknowledges a passionate desire akin to Olga's. Such glimpses of similarity contribute importantly to Denise's new understanding of Olga and to the reconciliation it makes possible.

The change in the poet's view of Olga is apparent in changes in her imagery. The flames of Olga's passion fade, as the poet comes to see clearly "that kind candle" in her sister's heart; recognizing that love was the source of Olga's rage, Denise now wonders, with some awe, "what kept compassion's candle alight in you . . . ?" (p. 60). Similarly, the image of relentlessly flowing water becomes first "a sea/of love and pain," (p. 57) and finally the streams and brooks through which Denise sees Olga's eyes and fully recognizes her sister.

New motifs also reflect and contribute to Denise's changing view of Olga. The most important of these is music. Gradually, we come to see Olga as a musician and lover of music. In the final poem, Denise recalls her sister "savagely" playing "straight through all the Beethoven sonatas," and realizes that Olga was playing to survive: "you were enduring in the/falls and rapids of the music, the arpeggios rang out, the rectory/trembled, our parents seemed effaced" (p. 59–60). The poet is able to recognize the importance of music to Olga here because she has earlier recalled a serener music which still binds her to Olga:

> *In a garden grene* [sic] *whenas I lay* —
> You set the words to a tune so plaintive

> it plucks its way through my life as through a wood.
>
> As through a wood, shadow and light between birches,
> gliding a moment in open glades, hidden by thickets of holly
>
> your life winds in me.
>
> *(Sorrow Dance*, p. 57)

The memory of this music leads directly to an extended memory of shared childhood longings and secrets, in which the age difference again dissolves; Olga's song twines through this memory, too: she had imagined that the sisters might lift a trapdoor in the ground and travel to "another country,"

> where we would live without father or mother
> and without longing for the upper world. *The birds*
> *sang sweet*, O song, *in the midst of the daye,*
> . . . . . . . .
> and we entered silent mid-Essex churches on hot afternoons
> and communed with the effigies of knights and their ladies
>
> and their slender dogs asleep at their feet,
> the stone so cold —          *In youth*
>
> *is pleasure, in youth is pleasure.*
>
> *(Sorrow Dance*, p. 58)

The sisters dream of freedom from adults, and of romance. Olga, too — it is her story, we're told — may have yearned to stay a child. Yet Olga's suffering, in childhood as later, runs as an undercurrent even of this most peaceful poem. Music, recollected, then, restores and enlarges the intimacy of which it was earlier an integral part.

Gradually, the poet's view of Olga changes. She recognizes Olga's suffering more fully as she sees her sister as a child, both in the dreamy passage just quoted, and in the painful passage that precedes her final vision: "I think of your eyes in that photo, six years before I was born,/the fear in them. What did you do with your fear,/later?" (p. 60). Acknowledging Olga's childhood, Denise herself matures. Recalling Olga's music, she finds another source of kinship in art. Recognizing this bond between them, recreating Olga, and through her sister's influence eventually expanding the possibilities of her own poetry, Levertov the poet indeed acts like Olga, the storyteller who attempted to recreate the world.

Levertov's new understanding and sense of kinship with Olga are confirmed in the final lines of the sequence. She recalls the past, when her eyes "smarted in pain and anger" at the thought of Olga; now, at the end, she says, "so many questions my eyes/smart to ask your eyes." (pp. 59–60). Finally, she returns to the imagery of the first poem, re-evoking Olga's warm sensuous darkness:

> . . . your eyes, gold brown eyes,
> the lashes short but the lids
> arched as if carved out of olivewood, eyes with some vision

of festive goodness in back of their hard, or veiled, or shining,
unknowable gaze . . . (Levertov's ellipsis)

(*Sorrow Dance*, p. 60)

By now the vision has gained the depth and intimacy of adult understanding
and love, which allow the speaker to acknowledge her own limits, and her
sister's integrity, and to accept the fact that some questions will never be answered.

Coming to terms with Olga, accepting and loving her, is important to the
poet in several ways. That this relationship was long weighted with misunder-
standing and pain is evident in Levertov's earlier, less direct, references to
it. In "Relative Figures Reappear" and "A Map of the Western Part of the
County of Essex in England," she refers to Olga as frightening but dear.[3] Two
other poems, "Song for a Dark Voice" and "A Window," evoke Olga's spirit
through imagery similar to that of the "Olga Poems" and surround that spirit
with a mysterious attraction.[4]

Another dimension of Olga's importance, transcending personal emotion
(but growing from it), is evident in the place this sequence takes in the center
of *The Sorrow Dance*, where it links poems of Eros, which explore sensuous
experience, first to poems that emphasize vision, elaborating on the new capacity for understanding achieved through reconciliation with Olga, and then,
most significantly, to poems of ardent political commitment. Levertov is
known today for her commitment to the anti-war and anti-nuclear movements. I believe that she owes the conviction that makes her political beliefs
integral to much of her writing to Olga and to her own effort to understand
the importance of her sister and their relationship. Before *The Sorrow Dance*,
her poetry does not generally reflect her political interests. That Olga has freed
her to speak out is clearly suggested in poems that follow the "Olga Poems."
In "A Note to Olga (1966)," the poet detects her sister's presence at a protest
march: "Your high soprano/sings out from just/in back of me—." It seems
to be Olga who is lifted "limp and ardent" into the gaping paddywagon (*Sorrow Dance*, pp. 88–89). We can also see Olga's influence in later books, most
notably *To Stay Alive*, and *The Freeing of the Dust*.[5] Her influence is present
both in Levertov's political topics and in her ability to sympathize with radical
protesters, some of whom are surely much more like Olga than like the poet
herself.

Olga's life is vindicated and honored in her sister's poems. Her passionate
commitment to change contributes to Levertov's maturity and her poetic development. Olga's pain, shared by Denise, gives depth to the latter's vision.
Levertov acknowledges her debt by concluding *The Sorrow Dance* with "The
Ballad of My Father," a poem written by Olga shortly before her death. Allowing Olga thus to speak for herself, she shares her book with her sister and
confirms the link between them.

But while Denise acknowledges that she has grown through her new understanding of Olga, herself, and their relationship, important differences remain, and Denise's view of life is validated. Olga's led her to grief and death. Denise's view, on the other hand, is echoed in the structure and process of the "Olga" sequence itself. Instead of "flowing" relentlessly, the poems, and with them the poet's view of Olga, unfold. The movements backward in time to a more intimate past, and even to the image of Olga's frightened face, can be thought of as the folding back of layers to reveal the essential core of Olga's character and the sisters' bond. Levertov also insists on the differences between them in the political poems of *To Stay Alive*: Olga has freed the poet to a fuller knowledge of Eros, but her fuller understanding means she must diverge from Olga's path, as she does when she turns away from consuming anger to affirm the value of struggling for life.

The final words of the "Olga Poems," then, are true both to Denise's love for her sister and to her recognition that Olga will always be inaccessible to her: that "unknowable gaze" is beautiful but impenetrable. Levertov thus acknowledges the tension of the sisters' bond, the contrast between intimacy and estrangement, which is one of Adrienne Rich's dominant themes when she explores the same subject.

Like Levertov, Rich portrays a changing relationship between sisters. Their explorations, however, are in many ways quite different. Levertov's "Olga Poems" are distinctively personal history; Rich's poems rarely concentrate so entirely on the personal, and some may be autobiographical only indirectly, if at all. Typically, Rich integrates several kinds of sisterhood, such as her own relationship with her biological sister, the sisterhood of female history, and archetypal images of sisters. Levertov's partly elegiac sequence moves toward an identifiable conclusion. Rich's poems, in contrast, concern a process that is ongoing both on the personal level and in a broader context.

Two elements implicit in Levertov's examination of the sisters' bond are treated more explicitly in Rich's. First is the problem of parents. Levertov twice refers to Olga's attempted "effacing" of their parents but she chooses only to suggest the possible implications. Rich, on the other hand, emphasizes sisters' relationships with their own parents, particularly their mothers, or shows them under the power of parents, especially that of "the fathers." Second, Rich finally makes explicit what Levertov implies even in her earliest insistence on the differences between herself and Olga: The sister is "who I might once have been."[6]

Rich's and Levertov's explorations of sisterhood also have important elements in common. For each, her sister has not only immediate personal importance but also metaphorical significance. While Olga seems to have a muse-like function, Rich's sister represents both an aspect of her self and the possibility of realizing a relationship among all women. Both poets are concerned with the paradox of intimacy and strangeness between sisters. And both ultimately acknowledge an uncertainty that outlasts all their love and effort, as they face the sister's "hard, or veiled, or shining,/unknowable gaze." Recognizing the sister's likeness to herself, each must also recognize the sister's inviolable integrity.

Rich describes her poetry as process and experience.[7] Her poems about sisters reflect and embody a developing understanding of herself, her sister, and her relationships to other women—a process that parallels and reflects the movement of Rich's work as a whole toward new visions of women.

The poems to be discussed here trace a process that begins in oppression and estrangement, then moves to a dreamlike, almost mythic vision that makes possible Rich's first extended analysis of the relationship between sisters. At this point the sisters are more fully realized individuals, the intense emotion involved in their bond is acknowledged, and they are seen in relation to their mother and to women's historical roles. The next poems take the sisters first into the wholly personal realm, and then personal closeness makes possible a fuller sense of historical connections among women. Most recently, Rich has turned to questions that must persist in an evolving relationship compounded of sameness and difference.

Rich only implies a sister relationship in the title of "A Woman Mourned by Daughters" (*Poems Selected and New*, p. 57).[8] The daughters are united by their estrangement from their dead mother, who has restrained, burdened, and betrayed them. For Rich, sisters united only as these daughters are have not achieved true sisterhood. In "Sisters" (*Poems Selected and New*, p. 61), Rich implies that estrangement between sisters is inevitable. In both of these poems Rich conveys a sense of emptiness in what might have been intimate, sustaining relationships. This sense of failure and estrangement reappears in a later poem, "A Primary Ground" (*Poems Selected and New*, pp. 203–204), where "your wife's twin sister," speechless and dying, represents the wife's own otherwise unacknowledged suffering, and the estrangement, in conventional patriarchal marriage, of the wife from herself and of sisters from each other. The fact that this poem comes later than others that depict advances in sisterhood indicates how slowly sisterly closeness grows; the fact that it is addressed to a man suggests a growing understanding of some of the sources of sisterly estrangement.

In her first step toward sisterly closeness, in "Flesh and Blood," Rich moves back into memories of childhood:

> Everyone else I've had to tell how it was,
> only not you.
> . . . . . . . .
> Doors slammed. We
> fell asleep, hot Sundays, in our slips,

two mad little goldfish

fluttering in a drying pond.
Nobody's seen the trouble I've seen
but you.
Our jokes are funnier for that
you'd say
and, Lord, it's true.

(*Leaflets*, p. 14)

Despite the humor, the relationship is limited: the little girls can only fall asleep. And their adult jokes are only a means of coping with trouble, not changing whatever caused it. In fact what makes this relationship strong also limits it: the sisters don't have to explain their pasts to each other, but we must wonder what will happen if they find, in the future, that they must do more than joke.

Rich begins to develop the fuller understanding of sisterhood that will eventually allow her to speak more profoundly to her sister as she moves, in "Women," into the world of symbol. In this realm she is able to see more clearly: "My three sisters are sitting/on rocks of black obsidian./For the first time, in this light, I can see who they are." (*Poems Selected and New*, pp. 109–110). Albert Gelpi refers to these sisters as "three images of self";[9] we can also take them to represent three images of one sister, and of female possibility. The mythic and symbolic quality of the vision is created by the starkness of the scene, the elemental contrasts of sea and rock, red and black, and the designation of the women as simply "my first sister," "my second sister," and "my third sister." The first two sisters are sewing; pain dominates their tasks: the first sews a costume in which "all her nerves will be visible"; the second sews "the seam over her heart which has never healed entirely." The third is gazing "at a dark red crust spreading westward far out on the sea./Her stockings are torn but she is beautiful." If the sewing sisters suggest the Fates, the third suggests the seer and the quester. The first two acknowledge pain; the third anticipates release and recreation for women as individuals and as sisters.

The imagery of "Women" is illuminated by the poems that precede it. In "5:30 A.M." (*Poems Selected and New*, pp. 106–107), Rich meditates on "The fox, panting, fire-eyed,/gone to earth in my chest." Speaker and fox are beautiful, "with our auburn/pelts, our trail of blood." Again, in "Abnegation" (*Poems Selected and New*, pp. 108–109), the red fox, "every hair on her pelt alive," is contrasted to the Scottish Convenanters, who "left me a westerness/a birthright, a red-stained, ravelled/afghan of sky."

Like the fox, the sister with the torn stockings has traveled over sharp terrain and may be bleeding. What she sees as she gazes out to sea, the "dark-red crust," is both the fading sun of the adamant covenanters, and the periodic blood of life, which unites the poet to the fox and to her sisters. Her vision of survival and rediscovered power makes the third sister beautiful, as it gives hope that the sisterly bond might be recreated in beauty and strength.

The possibility of such recreation is explored further in "The Mirror in Which Two Are Seen as One" (hereafter, "The Mirror," *Poems Selected and New*, pp. 193–195); again, the sister can be taken as both the speaker's blood sister and a part of herself, and by extension of both, as representing the possibility of sustaining relationships among all women.[10] The personal element is present in details of gesture and appearance and in the overt presence of emotion. This personal element contributes to the impression that the speaker is addressing herself, as well as others who share the experience. At the same time, the quality of dream or myth also persists, in the absence of ordinary, realistic explanations and connections, and the dream of birth, in which mother and sisters merge and are transformed. The personal and dream-like mythic qualities are equally essential. The "mirror" of recognition is created by the sisters' personal attention to each other, while the dream-vision of rebirth reveals in that mirror the possibility of recreating the self, in and through the sisterly relationship.

The first section of the poem contrasts her sister's competence in the kitchen to the speaker's sickness there, and the two seem hopelessly at odds. Happily, part 2 contradicts this. The first line, repeated from part 1, promises another chance: "She is the one you call sister." Now the speaker is active and competent. In contrast to the speaker's lightning blaze, and moderating it, is her sister's quiet beauty. Now, though, instead of opening an unbridgeable gap, their differences create an opportunity for generosity and a mutual responsiveness. Each can give something to the other, and in recognizing this they are unified: "you hand her a record/of two flutes in India reciting."

This new recognition and unity, within the self and between the sisters, is the "mirror" of part 3, which gives the speaker a new opportunity to define herself and her relationships with other women, including her sister. This opportunity will entail pain and uncertainty, but will also allow her to live. At the end of this poem the speaker has reached a beginning, with the prospect of rebirth. She has moved beyond "gazing," with the third sister of "Women," to actively "learning her trade," and the active mode of exploration will continue in the sister poems that follow this one.

Two of Rich's recent poems on sisters seem more explicitly autobiographical than those discussed so far. Having moved toward a vision of new possibilities for sister and self in "The Mirror," she can now examine directly the particular past shared with her sister Cynthia, to acknowledge their differences, and to explore the possibilities offered by the past, as well as the present and the future. In "Blood Sister" (*Poems Selected and New*, pp. 222–223), she addresses her sister directly for the first time since "Flesh and Blood." Now, instead of questioning their ability to know one another, as she had in "Sisters," she recollects their knowledge in a series of images evocative of the shared past. This recollection provides the foundation for a continuing relationship: The sisters see their childhood world diminished, but their own bond continues to grow:

> we sit at your table drinking coffee
> light flashes off unwashed sheetglass
> you are more beautiful than you have ever been
>
> . . . . . . . .
> ice fits itself around each twig of the lilac
> like a fist of law and order
> your imagination burns like a bulb in the frozen soil
> (*Poems Selected and New*, p. 223)

Although in "The Mirror" the speaker gave books, words, and music to her less articulate sister, here both speak, and the sister's imagination confirms that she is a person like the speaker herself, an equal in a relationship of mutual recognition, support, and inspiration. The strength of the sisters' bond allows Rich to contemplate the future with assurance, as the poem ends:

> when summer comes the ocean may be closed for good
> we will turn
> to the desert
> where survival
> takes naked and fiery forms
> (*Poems Selected and New*, p. 223)

Like "The Mirror," this poem ends by anticipating the future. The next poem, "Sibling Mysteries" (*The Dream of a Common Language*, pp. 47–52), takes the sisters deep into the past, to the foundations of that hope and the bedrock need for re-creation, as Rich integrates their personal history with the long history of sisters' common experience.

The poem's first four sections search out a female past, with an urgency evidenced in the poet's repeated plea, "Remind me." Part 1 looks back to prehistoric female experience: "Remind me how we walked/trying the planetary rock." Part 2 recounts the daughters' memories of the mother, the timeless experience of love, betrayal, and loss: "and how we thought she loved/the strange male body first." In the next section, part 3, Rich reaches out to embrace female communal experience: "we told/among ourselves our secrets, . . . / . . . piercing our lore in quilted galaxies." In part 4, she affirms the strength of female bonds when the outer forms of community are severed, and outcast women carry their "mother-secrets" to death, at the stake or adrift "in boats of skin on the ice-floe." Recalling "how sister gazed at sister/reaching through mirrored pupils/back to the mother," Rich envisions a spiritual link that transcends separation and death.

Rich has been addressing her own sister, and through her the sisterhood of shared experience. By evoking that long past, she has tried to build a foundation for their relationship, to strengthen their bond in the encircling arms and mirroring gaze of all who have preceded them, to find a common ground on which to transcend their differences. The memory of how sisters comforted each other even in the ultimate separation now brings her, at the beginning of part 5, to confront the distance between herself and Cynthia. They seem to have lost that knowledge of one another that Rich has evoked from the past: "*I feel acutely that we are strangers, my sister and I. . . . I don't know what really gives her pain or joy, nor does she know how I am happy or how I suffer.*" But then she travels back from the differences to their shared beginnings: "yet our eyes drink from each other/our lives were driven down the same dark canal."

The recognition of shared beginnings is the basis for her perception of a new old "truth," which Rich now believes can be the foundation of a true sisterly bond. Having "returned so far" into female history, she sees "the house of childhood," of their personal differences and of the patriarchal world in which they grew, as "absurd." Her rediscovery of a personal, primordial, and historic past enables her to deny the differences that have separated her from her sister and to assert a bond based on the sameness of their experience: "The daughters never were/true brides of the father"; rather, they were "brides of the mother/then brides of each other/under a different law." Her new assurance is evident in the poem's last line; no longer asking her sister to "Remind me," she is now able to embrace and give comfort: "Let me hold and tell you."

"Sibling Mysteries" marks several advances in Rich's imagination of sisterhood. She has transformed the vision of the mother presented in "A Woman Mourned by Daughters"; this transformation makes love between mother and daughter imaginable and creates the possibility of a strong sister bond. She has given an historical context to the relationships between men and women in patriarchy, which she criticized in "A Primary Ground," and has at the same time broken the silence that trapped the dying twin sister in that poem. The intimacy that she achieves in "Blood-Sister" and attempts to make more inclusive here, and the assurance with which she finally speaks, contrast her questions and her virtual dismissal of her sister in "Sisters." Exploring beyond the powerful but incomplete images of "Women," she has more fully imagined the sources of power that may free her and her sister from the pain of the earlier poem's first two sisters, as it enables them more clearly to imagine the vision of the third sister. As for Levertov, reclaiming past closeness enables Rich to transcend present alienation.

Rich concludes "Sibling Mysteries" by virtually denying differences between sisters and between women. This is an effective strategy in the struggle to affirm women's bonds, but questions persist that must eventually be dealt with if sisters and women are to build sustaining relationships based on recognition of the different truths of their individual lives. These questions concern the extent to which assertions of sameness are compatible with the desire to connect with all women, and the meanings and limits in individual women's lives of the "different law" Rich announces at the end of "Sibling Mysteries."

Perhaps having gained strength from the closeness established in "Sibling Mysteries," Rich begins, sometimes indirectly, to confront such questions in several of the poems of *A Wild Patience Has Taken Me This Far*. "Transit" (*A Wild Patience*, pp. 19–20) seems on the one hand to refer to the speaker and her sister (not necessarily to Rich and her blood sister); on the other hand, as in "Women," the two women may represent contrary elements of one self—reminding us, as did "The Mirror," of the link between sisterhood and self-knowledge: "Transit" emphasizes persistent differences: one woman is strong, the other is weak; one walks and skis, the other stands still, crippled. The possibility of a relationship between them (or of wholeness within the self) is not absolutely negated, yet the dominant impression is of questions inarticulated and unanswered and a relationship (or an identity: compare "Upper Broadway," *The Dream of a Common Language*, p. 41) as yet incomplete. The poem ends by implicitly admitting that women can't rely on the past alone to bind them together, that instead they must choose and create sisterhood. This realization opens the way for more uncertainty, reflected in the complicated and difficult syntax of the final stanza.

> When sisters separate they haunt each other
> as she, who I might once have been, haunts me
> or is it I who do the haunting
> halting and watching on the path
> how she appears again through lightly blowing
> crystals, how her strong knees carry her,
> how unaware she is, how simple
> this is for her, how without let or hindrance
> she travels in her body
> until the point of passing, where the skier
> and the cripple must decide
> to recognize each other?
>                    (*A Wild Patience*, pp. 19–20)

In "For Ethel Rosenberg" (*A Wild Patience*, pp. 26–30), "Heroines" (*A Wild Patience*, pp. 33–36), "For Memory" (*A Wild Patience*, pp. 21–22), and "Grandmothers" (*A Wild Patience*, pp. 37–39), Rich contemplates relationships with other women, some personally known to her, some historical. With all of them, she seems to seek a closer sisterhood, like that evoked in "Sibling Mysteries." And in each case, more directly than in "Transit," she raises questions about the nature and effects of differences among women and how they can be bridged.

These poems reveal Rich's renewed awareness of differences between sisters and women and her desire to avoid betraying others by imposing her own experiences and perceptions on them. In "Transit," this was suggested less directly by the sister's "cap of many colors," which reminded us of Joseph's coat and his betrayal by his brothers. The circle of sisterhood has widened, but now Rich recognizes the limits of likeness and more fully acknowledges the individual integrity of the women with whom she seeks intimacy. Difficult questions accompany sisterhood on the large scale as well as between individual blood sisters. This recognition and the resulting uncertainty recall Levertov's situation at the end of the "Olga Poems," when having discovered their likenesses, she finally still faces Olga's "unknowable gaze."

Like Levertov's, Rich's sister poems are also linked by recurring imagery and motifs. The mirror and childbirth imply the two major types of metaphoric meaning that the sister has for Rich. First, despite the fact that they may be in some respects strangers to each other, the sister represents a part of the self; knowing the sister, seeing oneself in her and her in oneself, becomes a way of knowing oneself. Second, the bond with the sister who is both strange and familiar is a prototype for and a validation of the connections among all women that Rich has been struggling to forge through most of her career. The sister, then, for Rich as for Levertov, is central to the poet's most vital task and commitment; she represents the link between the personal and the political.

A third unifying element in Rich's sister poems is the theme of language, which links these poems to another of Rich's dominant concerns. Exploring sisterhood is yet another way of learning to speak truly and freely. These poems move from unanswered questions, silence, and failed language to language that both falters and then redeems in "The Mirror." Language works for the sisters in "Blood Sister," and in "Sibling Mysteries," the sisters' mutual confirmation and retelling of the past is essential to the shared future Rich imagines. This development also suggests another parallel with Levertov, who, having recreated the bond with her sister, also gained new language in the capacity to write on new topics.

Like Levertov, Rich emphasizes the paradox of likeness and difference between sisters. The recognition of likeness enables each to know herself and her relationship to others through knowing her sister. The recognition of difference, once the common ground has been recovered, brings a sense of mystery, of the limits of relationship, and of the need to protect one's own and one's sister's integrity. Together, these recognitions make the sisters' bond an evolving, rather than a static, relationship. Both Rich and Levertov demonstrate the vision, understanding, and strength to be gained for woman and poet in the exploration of that bond.

## NOTES

1. Denise Levertov, "The Olga Poems." *The Sorrow Dance* (New York: New Directions, 1966), 53–60 (Hereafter, *Sorrow Dance*). I had completed this essay before I became aware of Paul Lacey's chapter on Levertov in *The Inner War* (Philadel-

phia: Fortress Press, 1972). He analyzes the "Olga Poems" as reflecting the poet's reconciliation with a forerunner, without focusing on the sister relationship. Our discussions thus complement each other.

2. Linda W. Wagner sees Olga as fearing death, but her concern with the slums and her ghostly presence at a protest march later suggest that we might more justly describe her as resisting the human acceptance of death that supports poverty and war. Wagner, *Denise Levertov* (New York: Twayne, 1967), 112–114.

3. Denise Levertov, *Collected Earlier Poems* (New York: New Directions, 1979), 124–125; and *The Jacob's Ladder* (New York: New Directions, 1961), 19–20.

4. Levertov, *The Jacob's Ladder*, 23–24.

5. Denise Levertov, *The Freeing of the Dust* (New York: New Directions, 1975); and *To Stay Alive* (New York: New Directions, 1971).

6. Adrienne Rich, "Transit," *A Wild Patience Has Taken Me This Far* (New York: Norton, 1981), 19–20.

7. See "Poetry and Experience: Statement at a Poetry Reading, 1964," in *Adrienne Rich's Poetry*, eds. Barbara C. Gelpi and Albert Gelpi (New York: Norton, 1975), 89; and Rich's Foreword to *Poems Selected and New* (New York: Norton, 1975), xv.

8. Page numbers for all poems quoted from the following books will be given in parentheses in the text: *Poems Selected and New* (New York: Norton, 1975); *Leaflets* (New York: Norton, 1969); *The Dream of a Common Language* (New York: Norton, 1978); and *A Wild Patience Has Taken Me This Far* (New York: Norton, 1981).

9. Albert Gelpi, "Adrienne Rich: The Poetics of Change," in *American Poetry Since 1960*, ed. Robert B. Shaw (Cheadle, Cheshire: Carcanet Press, Ltd., 1973); reprinted in *Adrienne Rich's Poetry*, 147.

10. I am indebted for much of my understanding of this poem to Susan R. Van Dyne's "The Mirrored Vision of Adrienne Rich," *Modern Poetry Studies* 8 (1977): 140–173. Van Dyne does not, however, discuss the poem's implications for the sister bond.

# 10 Current Sisters Speak About Their Bonds

Toni A. H. McNaron

Betty McNaron McAllister (1960)

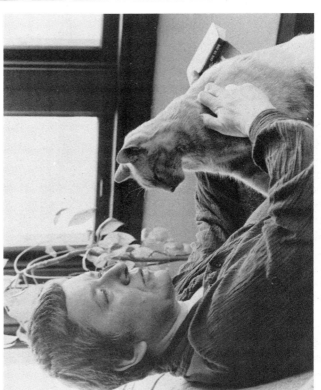

Toni McNaron (1979)
Photographed by Linda Neils

The connection between blood sisters continues to intrigue, move, and vex many living women, both those who have such ties in their own families and those who don't. In researching this book, I sent out some fifty questionnaires (see sample in Appendix), asking contemporary pairs of sisters to respond to questions about the history of their feelings for each other and about factors that have separated them and drawn them closer. My sample included black and white sisters, old and young sisters, and sisters living all over the United States. The results show significant parallels between the historic pairs discussed in this volume and women making sense of their relationships in the present.

I was particularly interested in those things that had divided and united the sisters, since I wondered how they would compare to the stories included here. The unifiers most often given include children, feminism, trouble with one or more husbands or lovers, alcoholism in a close family member, the shared world of childhood, illness either in a parent or one of them, death of one or more parents. Some less-frequently cited but no less significant unifying factors include participation in the nuclear freeze, support for chosen work and self-development, intense interest in such external matters as clothes, art, literature, films, food, holidays, a home town or state, the beach, a cousin, a brother. Several felt drawn together by a shared cultural or biological factor, i.e., Judaism, being Black, being twins, being lesbians. One pair had found new closeness when they collaborated on a creative project in which each one's talent was crucial. Another believed that a long-standing but healthy sense of competition had united them as they formed a kind of buffer against other outside difficulties. Several respondents listed a deep context of family love and comfort, while one woman cited her and her sister's shared experience of incest within their family as a major ground for unity.

When asked to articulate what caused separation or division between themselves and their sisters, women most often cited such factors as envy and jealousy most often over a parent, lack of basic trust in the other sister, religion, choice of life-style, difference in personality types (one being an introvert, the other an extravert), a family pattern of silence that kept them from learning much about their sister, large age differences, money issues, lack of interest in each other's daily lives, separation by geographical distance, an inability to express feelings with one another, and competition. Other explanations, cited less often, include clashing over modes of handling such family crises as a divorce, death of a parent, a spouse's alcoholism, the experience of incest within the family of origin; the fact of being twins; a fundamental lack of respect for a sister and/or her way of living her daily life; jealousy over who was thinner, prettier, better able to "fit in" in the family.

Since the same events figure as agents for unity and division, it seems clear that what matters is how sisters handle such occurrences. I am also struck by the force of externals in these women's lives, reminding us all that our personal experiences cannot escape the institutional and social structures around us.

Those completing the questionnaires were asked to trace their feelings about their sisters from childhood, through adolescence, and into the present. Most respondents felt the most competitive and/or alienated during adolescence and young adulthood, suggesting that sisterhood does not overcome the natural pressures of that tumultuous era in a person's life. However, many voice relief or pleasure over the fact that in more recent years, they and their sisters have mended enough of their fences to have a warm relationship. A few express a reversal of this pattern: in childhood and adolescence they felt adoration, care, protective feelings toward their sisters, only to be pulled apart by later decisions and value differences. These women say or imply their hurt and even bitterness that such is the case, and wish things could be different so that they and their sisters could be more closely connected.

Of those who responded to the following question — "If you also have a brother, what are some similarities and some differences in your history and present feelings toward him as compared with your sister?" — the majority conclude that their relationship with their brother has been and remains smoother. However, many say that this smoothness is accompanied by a less strong bond or by less intense emotions toward their brother. A few comment on their preference for relating to their male sibling, since their automatic differences keep them at an emotional distance which insures a more uniform pattern of relating.

The most fascinating responses came from the question: "How would you characterize this relationship [with your sister] in comparison with other women friends in your life?" Responses ranged from those who found their nonblood friendships altogether more gratifying to those who concluded that they held all other bonds with women up against a virtually incomparable tie with their sisters. Some who define themselves as feminists say that things are so much simpler with their chosen women friends, since they can pick people with like minds, whereas their sisters are given to them through family and must then be coped with regardless of the gulfs that may exist between them. But the single most repeated response can be mirrored in this statement from one woman in her thirties whose sister is extremely important to her: "The permanence and long history create a unique bond for me. On the other hand, there are basic things we never talk much about. Also I suspect some differences are so great that if we weren't sisters, we might never have been friends." This fundamental ambivalence reflects the pattern found in almost all the stories in this collection.

The current sisters also confirm another thread found in the stories here, namely that learning how to relate to one's sister can be instrumental in all subsequent relationships. As one response on a questionnaire put it: "I have loved some women more passionately [than I have my sister] because of their differences from me and probably because of the incest taboo, but my sisters have remained beloved longest. They allowed me to trust and love women as my parents did. But the sisters helped me to learn how to treat friends, how to be disinterested, to love who friends become, to work in groups with women, to support women. Theirs is a steadiness which mirrors what I think I have in my marriage — it grows and is lifelong. We are connected. They are the river which supports me and my other women friends as we float and swim along." Christina Rossetti or Virginia Woolf or the Abbott sisters would nod wisely if they could read such words; and if Robin Fast's thesis is correct, so would Denise Levertov and Adrienne Rich.

Questions that remain unanswered include these: What do sisters mean to each other if they grow up as part of an oppressed group within their culture? What do sisters do with their erotic fantasies and feelings for one another, and what is the correlation between this phenomenon and their pulls toward compulsory heterosexuality within the society? What is lost to the women who cannot find their way back to their blood sisters in terms of their capacity or willingness to form intimate relations with any other women? Why is a failed relation with one's sister so excruciatingly painful no matter how long ago it may have set in? If only one sister becomes known by the public world, how does the other one feel about her role and function?

When all these and many other questions have been explored and even answered, we still may not have the key to the intensity that lies at the core of so many sisters' feelings for one another. From my own experience and from the stories told here, I have suggested that it has something to do with the strange familiarity felt by sisterly pairs. Surely there are countless sisters who may not respond to this explanation, but I hope that countless more will find something of themselves in what they read. And for those who disagree with my analysis, I hope you will give voice to your own in whatever form suits you. For I am convinced that women related to one another in this way have profound stories to tell, first of all to each other, and then to the rest of us building a network across our differences. I offer this collection as my own best contribution to the dialogue.

# Appendix

Name _____

Address _____

Your Age _____       Your Sister's Age _____

What is your present relationship to your sister?


What issues have divided you and your sister?


What issues have united you and your sister?


How did you feel about your sister when you were a little girl (pre-12)?


How did you feel about your sister when you were a teenager?


How would you characterize this relationship in comparison with others in your family of origin?


How would you characterize this relationship in comparison with other women friends in your life?


If you also have a brother, what are some similarities and some differences in your history and present feelings toward him as compared with your sister?


Feel free to use additional space for any of these questions. Any additional comments you may wish to make will be welcome. Thank you for participating in this questionnaire. I want to say again that I will not attribute anything you say by name or other distinguishing information.

# Index

# About the Contributors

LELA B. COSTIN is a professor in the School of Social Work at the University of Illinois. She is the author of *Child Welfare: Policies and Practices*, is co-author of *Contemporary Social Work*, and has published extensively in professional journals. She is currently working on a study of historical influences on the development of public policy with respect to child neglect and abuse.

DIANE D'AMICO is an assistant professor at Allegheny College in Meadville, Pennsylvania. She has published articles on Christina Rossetti in *Victorian Poetry, Victorians Institute Journal, The Journal of Pre-Raphaelite Studies*, and the *University of Dayton Review*.

CELIA M. ECKHARDT loves to write and to lecture. She enjoys Chaucer, Louise Bogan, Alice Walker. She has published a biography of Fanny Wright called *Fanny Wright: Rebel in America* (Harvard University Press, 1984) about which she says "Fanny Wright changed my life and I have become a political activist in women's causes."

ROBIN RILEY FAST teaches composition and American literature at the University of Akron. Her special interests are in nineteenth century literature and women in literature. She has published articles on Dickinson, Whitman, and George Eliot.

SUSAN S. LANSER teaches literature and women's studies at Georgetown University. She has written *The Narrative Act: Point of View in Prose Fiction* (1982) and is presently completing a book entitled *Fictions of Authority: Women Writers and Narrative Voice*, which will include a discussion of Austen's novels.

TONI A. H. McNARON is a professor of English and Women's Studies at the University of Minnesota. She has co-edited *Voices in the Night: Women Speaking About Incest*, and published articles on Woolf, Hall, and gender development in her own life. She has recently completed an autobiography entitled *Comings Out*.

ADALAIDE MORRIS teaches at the University of Iowa. She has published a book on the poetry of Wallace Stevens and essays on the poetry of Dickinson, H. D., and Rich.

SYLVIA STRAUSS teaches women's history and English history at Kean College, New Jersey. She has written numerous articles and reviews, and is the author of "Traitors to the Masculine Cause: The Men's Campaigns for Women's Rights," 1982.